TAE KWON DO FOR WOMEN

JENNIFER LAWLER

D1408626

Wish
PUBLISHING

Wish Publishing
Terre Haute, Indiana
www.wishpublishing.com

LCCN: 00-107208

The author and the publisher assume no responsibility for any injury that may occur as a result of attempting to do any of the movements, techniques or exercises described in this book. These activities require strenuous physical activity and a physical examination is advisable before starting this or any other exercise activity.

Cover designed by Phil Velikan
Diagrams by J.P. Merz
Cover photography by PhotoDisc
Interior photography by Jennifer Lawler
Proofread by Heather Lowhorn

Printed in the United States of America
10 9 8 7 6 5 4 3 2 1

Published in the United States by
Wish Publishing
P.O. Box 10337
Terre Haute, IN 47801, USA
www.wishpublishing.com

Distributed in the United States by
Cardinal Publishers Group
Indianapolis, Indiana 46240

To my little one, Jessica the lionhearted.

ACKNOWLEDGMENTS

As usual, I must thank Mr. and Mrs. Donald Booth of New Horizons Black Belt Academy of Tae Kwon Do (Lawrence, Kansas), for their support and encouragement throughout the years. I must also thank Master Woo Jin Jung, without whom I never would have gotten this far.

My greatest appreciation to the Anderson family of black belts — Vickie, Chantal and Brian ("Chip") — who never fail to come to my rescue even with no notice at all.

Thanks to all of those martial artists who allowed me to take their photographs for this book: Susan Booth, Chantal Anderson, Vickie Anderson, Maggie Brooke, Emma Brooke, Brian "Chip" Anderson, J.P. Merz, Arash Yeganch and Bret Kay, who doubles as my husband and technical advisor.

Mr. Merz provided drawings even when I couldn't exactly explain what I wanted. I said, "You know what I mean," and he did.

TABLE OF CONTENTS

PART ONE:
WHAT IS TAE KWON DO?

1

INTRODUCTION TO TAE KWON DO

Tae Kwon Do, the Korean art of hand and foot fighting, captivates millions of practitioners throughout the world with its impressive high kicks and powerful attacking techniques. Yet, it is a defensive art. Committing to learning Tae Kwon Do means committing to the obligation to use it correctly. This requires an understanding of the background of Tae Kwon Do and its purpose as a way of life.

WHAT IS TAE KWON DO?

When first introducing Tae Kwon Do in the United States, teachers called it "Korean Karate," since Americans were familar with Japanese martial arts but not Tae Kwon Do.

Tae Kwon Do resembles Karate in some ways. Tae Kwon Do uses hand techniques, such as punches, but it emphasizes high kicks, jumping kicks and "flying" kicks. In fact, most people consider it a kicking art. The high kicks come from an older Korean martial art, whose practitioners had to fight against mounted warriors. Thus, the high kicks would knock a warrior off his horse—onto the ground, where the martial artist could more easily defeat him.

Tae Kwon Do is an empty-hand martial art, which means that it does not teach the use of weapons. This is in keeping with its history; for many years, their Japanese occupiers banned Koreans from owning weapons. Thus, Korean martial arts developed powerful techniques that did not require the use of weapons.

Tae Kwon Do is a defensive martial art. Although it is known for its aggressive offensive attacks, the practitioner is taught never to instigate a fight and to walk away whenever possible. White belts are instructed to say, "I don't want to fight," at least twice before responding to an attack with a physical reaction.

THE FOUNDER OF TAE KWON DO

General Hong-Hi Choi founded the modern art of Tae Kwon Do after World War II, when Korean nationalists attempted to rediscover cultural practices that had been driven underground during the lengthy Japanese occupation of their country. General Choi collected a variety of techniques from indigenous Korean martial arts, such as Taekyun and Subak, developed others to fill in the gaps, organized and systematized them, and began teaching Tae Kwon Do to Korean soldiers.

Tae Kwon Do draws from Chinese martial arts in its circular movements, joint locks, breathing exercises and certain throwing techniques. It draws from Japanese martial arts in its attacking techniques and vital point striking. Despite these strong influences, Tae Kwon Do is a unique martial art, challenging to master and fascinating to watch.

HISTORY OF KOREAN MARTIAL ARTS

Originally, empty-hand (weaponless) fighting systems came to Korea from T'ang Dynasty China. Korean warriors learned Subak and Taekyun, which they demonstrated in tournaments. In Silla Dynasty Korea, a group of noblemen developed a system for military leadership called Hwarang-do, which means "the way of the flowering youth." Like the feudal Samurai in Japan, the Hwarang (practitioners of Hwarang-do) learned martial skills, strategy, etiquette, Buddhism, and three main characteristics: loyalty, courage and justice.

Won Kang Bopsa, a Buddhist monk, is believed to have developed Taekyun, which he taught to the Hwarang. It soon became a fighting system that rivaled Japanese Karate and Chinese Kung-fu (also called, more properly, Wushu).

Over the next centuries, martial arts practice in Korea declined. The Koryo dynasty, which followed the Silla, emphasized intellectual pursuits over physical ones. Later, Mongol invaders prevented Koreans from practicing martial arts. Korean warriors took refuge in Buddhist monasteries and passed their martial arts knowledge on to a select few followers willing to learn.

In 1592, Japan invaded Korea. Korea relied on China for aid, and in the next centuries closed itself off from the outside world, becoming known as the Hermit Kingdom. Only the Chinese were permitted access to Korea, and their influence was paramount. Early in the twentieth century, Japan fought China for control of Korea, and in 1903, Japan conquered Korea. During their occupation, the Japanese prevented Koreans from passing on their culture. They could not teach the Korean language, nor could they practice their martial arts.

THE SPREAD OF TAE KWON DO

After the end of World War II, Korea gained independence from Japan and

Koreans began rediscovering many aspects of their culture. At this time, General Choi established Tae Kwon Do as an important feature of Korean culture. General Choi established the International Tae Kwon Do Federation (ITF) in order to oversee the art. This organization awards and recognizes black belt ranks and promotes the sport throughout the world.

In the late 1950s, a skilled Tae Kwon Do practitioner, Master Jhoon Rhee, emigrated from Korea to the United States and began teaching Tae Kwon Do to Americans. Although he called his martial art "Karate," it was really Tae Kwon Do. Today, Jhoon Rhee is called the father of American Tae Kwon Do.

Other teachers followed his example, and by the late 1980s, they had established thousands of Tae Kwon Do schools throughout the world. Now, almost every city and many smaller towns have at least one Tae Kwon Do school.

TAE KWON DO: A WAY OF LIFE

As General Choi originally envisioned it, Tae Kwon Do is meant to be an entire way of life, not simply a method of self-defense. Tae Kwon Do practitioners adhere to the Five Tenets of Tae Kwon Do, principles intended to build character and promote a civilized society. The Five Tenets are courtesy, integrity, perseverance, self-control, and indomitable spirit. Part of one's development in Tae Kwon Do stems from learning and understanding these principles.

Tae Kwon Do includes memorizing and performing hyung (forms), participating in step and freestyle sparring and practicing self-defense techniques. General Choi insisted that teachers who did not teach the moral aspects of Tae Kwon Do — that is, teachers who did not adhere to the Tenets and did not teach all elements of Tae Kwon Do — were not teachers at all. He discouraged practitioners from thinking of Tae Kwon Do as merely a sport or simply a way to keep in shape.

OTHER PHILOSOPHIES

Other teachers, however, disagreed. Many felt that the fighting techniques of Tae Kwon Do were so superior to other styles that they emphasized only this aspect. Some athletes train in Tae Kwon Do just as they would boxing — in order to participate in tournaments and to win sparring competitions. These pracitioners tend to emphasize the sport aspect of Tae Kwon Do and are more likely to be associated with the World Tae Kwon Do Federation (WTF), an organization that promotes Tae Kwon Do and sponsors Olympic athletes. WTF-style Tae Kwon Do is often called Olympic-style.

ITF-STYLE VERSUS WTF-STYLE

These two main styles differ in their emphasis. WTF-style emphasizes the sport aspect, particularly tournament sparring. The more traditional ITF style emphasizes a holistic approach, including forms, techniques practice, self-defense and sparring. The two styles differ in how they conduct and score sparring matches. ITF-style sparring matches are usually traditional point matches, where control, speed and variety of techniques win. In an ITF competition, a well-executed technique that is partially blocked or barely touches the competitor is considered superior to a poorly-executed technique that lands unblocked.

WTF-style sparring competition emphasizes heavier contact. For a point to count, a "trembling shock" must occur. This means the opponent must visibly move through space as a result of the kick or punch. For this reason, WTF-style fighters tend to rely on a few very powerful techniques. Any technique that is blocked, no matter how well-executed, does not score.

The styles also differ in the types of forms that are taught to students. WTF style teaches a series of forms different from the ITF, but the techniques are all the same.

THE TECHNIQUES OF TAE KWON DO

In addition to kicks and punches, Tae Kwon Do incorporates takedown techniques and throws, such as those used in Aikido and Judo. Joint locks and vital point strikes, similar to those in Jujutsu, also form part of the arsenal. In this way, Tae Kwon Do combines elements of many different martial arts, fusing them together to create a powerful fighting system.

Tae Kwon Do differs from other martial arts in its focus on board breaking. Practitioners use board breaking to demonstrate power, technique and mental discipline, often for the purpose of promotion testing, to compete in tournament competition or to demonstrate their skills to non-participants.

Most often, practitioners break one-inch pine boards, although black belts sometimes break concrete blocks. If a martial artist performs her technique correctly, the board (or block) will break. In fact, breaking can be quite easy. But the idea of board breaking, on the other hand, can be intimidating. Therefore, the mental aspect of board breaking is far more important than the physical aspect. Overcoming fear and uncertainty during board breaking helps Tae Kwon Do practitioners face opponents even though they may feel afraid.

PHYSICAL ELEMENTS

Tae Kwon Do does not rely only on physical techniques. Mental and even emotional aspects are equally important. Only through the correct harmony of mind, body and spirit can a true martial artist be born. Nonetheless, this book will focus on the physical aspects of Tae Kwon Do, since it is through the physical practice of Tae Kwon Do that the various elements fall into place.

Tae Kwon Do practice is typically divided into four areas: fighting techniques, forms, sparring and self-defense. These are interrelated. You can't focus on forms, for example, and expect to improve if you don't also practice sparring. The balance of all four areas makes you a better martial artist. This does not mean you won't be more skilled in some areas than in others or that you won't prefer one over another. But you can't ignore one area without jeopardizing the others.

FIGHTING TECHNIQUES

The first things you learn are the basic building blocks: punches, kicks, blocks and stances. You must learn and understand each technique individually before you can combine them together to create forms or to participate in sparring. Don't worry; it takes only a few short weeks to understand the basic techniques of Tae Kwon Do, although it will take years to master them. If you practice daily, you'll be competent in just a few months, regardless of your age, physical condition and previous athletic experience.

FORMS

Once you've learned the basic techniques of Tae Kwon Do, you will learn forms, sparring and self-defense. A form (called "hyung" in Korean) is a pattern of predetermined movements that you must memorize. Forms allow you to work on techniques in a series and to combine them together, so that they flow. A form also allows you to practice a number of techniques in a small amount of space. Forms emphasize grace, beauty, agility and timing.

At each stage of your martial arts training, you will learn at least one new form. Once you memorize a form, you must continue to practice it, even after you have learned other forms. Black belts can always perform beginner forms on demand because they practice them frequently.

Forms not only sharpen your physical skills, they sharpen your mental skills. By continually practicing the same set of techniques in a form, the form becomes rote. Because you don't have to think about what comes next, you are free to focus on each technique. Instead of analyzing, processing, theorizing and planning, you simply move from one technique to the next, trying to make each technique perfect. Thinking too much slows you down and impairs your reflexes. It allows doubt and indecision to creep in. Practicing forms allows your mind to focus on creating perfect techniques without thinking, "Is this the appropriate technique for this situation?"

As your skills develop, the forms you learn become more difficult and more demanding, both mentally and physically. But this challenge is necessary to your growth as a martial artist. Eventually, as a black belt, you can create your own forms.

SPARRING

Once you've learned the basic techniques of Tae Kwon Do, you can put them together in sparring. Tae Kwon Do uses two types of sparring: step sparring and freestyle sparring. In step sparring, you work with a partner under carefully controlled conditions. One partner attacks with one technique, such as a punch, while the other partner blocks the attack and counterattacks with one or more techniques. Because the attacking partner does not keep attacking, but instead waits for the other partner to defend and counterattack, step sparring is an ideal method of trying unfamiliar techniques with a partner and for learning how to put several techniques together.

In freestyle sparring, partners attack and defend as in an actual fight, although they follow special guidelines. Fighters wear safety gear, cannot strike to certain targets, and must use excellent control when they fight.

SELF-DEFENSE

Once you've learned a few basic fighting techniques, you're ready to learn to put them to use in a self-defense situation. Self-defense practice builds on realistic situations. For example, your partner will grab you by the arm, just as a mugger might on the street. You then respond using your self-defense knowledge.

You must practice self-defense techniques until they become automatic so that you don't freeze if you're ever confronted. Instead of wondering what you should do, you'll automatically respond to the attack with self-defense techniques appropriate to the situation.

Self-defense practice helps you become more confident in your ability to take care of yourself.

AN ENTIRE FIGHTING SYSTEM

Practicing fighting techniques, forms, sparring and self-defense makes you a well-rounded martial artist. Without careful attention to each area, your martial arts performance can suffer. Plan to spend equal amounts of time mastering each skill area.

2
BENEFITS OF TAE KWON DO TRAINING

When you ask a Tae Kwon Do practitioner why she practices Tae Kwon Do, the answer you get isn't likely to be the one you expect. You might expect to hear, "I like knowing I can defend myself and my family," or "I like the exercise," but you would be more likely to hear, "It increases my self-confidence," or "It helps me focus so that I can study better."

Practitioners of Tae Kwon Do reap many benefits — and not just physical ones. People of any age, size and physical condition can enjoy these benefits. Students as young as 4 or 5 can learn simple techniques and can be taught ethics as well as basic awareness of self-defense. Many older people can practice Tae Kwon Do — there are 70-year-olds still routinely working out.

Even if you have a physical disability, you can participate. Those who suffer chronic medical conditions such as asthma, cystic fibrosis, multiple sclerosis, muscular dystrophy and arthritis have successfully practiced Tae Kwon Do. Many people find that their symptoms become less severe with regular practice of Tae Kwon Do, and that the practice helps them overcome some of the challenges of the disease.

STRENGTH, AGILITY AND ENDURANCE

By practicing on a regular basis, you can become stronger and more agile, with greater endurance. When you begin practicing, you will find that your workout takes place in stops and starts, as you try to execute the techniques correctly. As you become more proficient, you will find that a Tae Kwon Do workout can be aerobic, effectively increasing your lung capacity and improving your cardiovascular health.

In addition, you will build strength through the repeated performance of techniques. Many Tae Kwon Do practitioners incorporate conditioning exercises into their workout to increase their strength — and thus, the power of their techniques. Others lift weights. Although this is not necessary, the more you concentrate on creating stronger techniques, the more powerful you'll become. Within the first few months of training, you will probably see an increase in strength and muscle tone (although not necessarily muscle *mass*; many women prefer not to bulk up and there is no special need to do so).

Tae Kwon Do requires flexibility and agility. Those with limited flexibility can still perform the techniques, improving their techniques as they gain more flexibility. If their flexibilty is limited for physical reasons, they can modify the techniques (such as by not performing high kicks) and still gain proficiency in Tae Kwon Do.

The more you practice, however, the more your flexibility improves. Women, who tend to be more flexible than men anyway, will often see dramatic increases in their flexibility. As you learn to do the high kicks and jumping techniques, your flexibility (as well as your strength) will increase. This allows you to do everyday activities more easily. You will be less prone to the strains and sprains that happen when your body is stiff, sore and out of shape.

MENTAL AND EMOTIONAL BENEFITS

Learning the techniques of Tae Kwon Do can make you feel more confident and more willing to take chances. You may become more assertive and stronger in all areas of life. Many women report that they stand up for themselves at work and home once they begin practicing martial arts. They believe they are more likely to say what they think.

Because practicing Tae Kwon Do improves your physical fitness, you may become more confident about your physical appearance. It also helps you appreciate strength and fitness as opposed to the unrealistically thin models women are expected to imitate. Women who practice Tae Kwon Do understand that frailty is not beautiful, and they become more comfortable with their own bodies, and thus, more self-confident.

As you learn martial arts techniques, you realize that you have to practice them repeatedly in order to remember them and to do them correctly. Because martial artists are highly motivated to learn their techniques, they develop the self-discipline necessary to practice frequently. Working on your skills even when you're tired increases your sense of self-discipline, which can apply to other areas of your life.

Tae Kwon Do practice helps you develop focus and concentration. Learning to do the techniques and then performing them correctly requires your full attention. This makes a martial arts workout the perfect antidote for a stressful day. Instead of collapsing on the sofa and feeling exhausted, you can work out and feel refreshed. Instead of dwelling on the things that went wrong today, or on all the things you have to do tomorrow, you must focus on the present. All you think about is what you're doing right this minute.

Such focus and concentration does not come right away. At first you will find your mind wandering as you try to perform a kick. But since success depends on focus, you'll learn to concentrate. Once you have the habit of concentrating your mind while you practice Tae Kwon Do, you will find that you can use that ability in other areas of life, even amid distractions.

All of these benefits of Tae Kwon Do develop through committment to the art and through frequent practice of all the elements of Tae Kwon Do.

3

DEVELOPING CHARACTER AND CHI

To become a true martial artist — and not just a person who knows a few fancy kicks — you must develop the characteristics that make you a better person. Tae Kwon Do students learn and follow the Five Tenets of Tae Kwon Do, a system of ethical behavior that helps develop character. If Tae Kwon Do is a way of life, then incorporating the Tenets into your daily life is part of the way of Tae Kwon Do.

THE FIVE TENETS OF TAE KWON DO

The Five Tenets interrelate. You must practice all of them — courtesy, integrity, perseverance, self-control and indomitable spirit — not just the one that appeals most to you.

Although you should practice these tenets in all areas of life (home, work, school), you must practice them in specific ways in the training hall. Once you've mastered practicing the Tenets when you're in the training hall, you'll begin to understand how they're used outside the training hall.

Courtesy

In the martial arts classroom, you show good manners by bowing to the instructor and other classmates and by using "sir" and "ma'am" when talking to instructors and senior students. This helps create an environment where your ego is not the most important thing in the room.

By being courteous, you show your respect. Instructors and senior students deserve your respect because of their committment to the art. Even if you can jump higher than a student who has been practicing longer, that student *has* been practicing longer, and that dedication should be respected.

Courtesy requires that you share your knowledge with others. Although you shouldn't teach the techniques without proper supervision, you should be willing to work with junior students so that they can benefit from what you've learned.

In the training hall, courtesy also means treating the art itself with respect. Thus, you shouldn't use your Tae Kwon Do knowledge unless it is absolutely necessary. And you shouldn't boast about your abilities or put yourself above the art.

Cultivating courtesy outside the training hall is more than just being polite and demonstrating your good manners. Just as Tae Kwon Do is a way of life, courtesy is a way of life, a way of looking at the world. For example, if someone cuts you off while you're driving, your first reaction might be to honk your horn or to try to retaliate by cutting that person off. But if you're courteous, you will neither honk nor cut the other person off. Even without martial arts training, it is easy to understand this concept.

However, true courtesy takes this a step further. True courtesy demands that you rethink such situations entirely. In Confucian philosophy (a philosophy that millions of Koreans adhere to) there are carefully regulated relationships between people, with elaborately detailed guidelines for conducting those relationships. In essence, Confucian philosophy says that if you have no relationship with another person, then you must be unaffected by what that person does. Your obligation is to maintain your own relationships (with your boss, your spouse, your children) in an appropriate way. All else does not require your energy and should be ignored.

Therefore, instead of wasting valuable energy becoming angry at the driver who cut you off, you must ignore the offense entirely. Further, you must not let it bother you. For someone not experienced in a Confucian mindset, this can be a challenge, but gaining control over your emotional responses prepares you for many difficulties.

Integrity

Integrity means committing to honest and ethical behavior. Most of us know someone who is the epitome of integrity. The idea of that person lying or stealing is impossible to imagine. The Tenet of Integrity asks us to be that kind of person.

In the training hall, you practice integrity in many ways. If you work out as hard as you can each time you train, you're practicing integrity. Instead of offering excuses for why you can't work as hard as you should, you practice as perfectly as possible each time you work out. Integrity means putting your greatest effort into each technique and movement you perform, even when no one else is watching. Many of us can work hard when someone is watching us, but it's another story when we're alone. If you get in the habit of lowering your expectations when no one is watching, you're not conducting your life with integrity.

Outside the training hall, you'll have many opportunities to practice integrity. Each day presents us with choices about how we plan to live. At work, you should put forth your best effort every day. You should take sick days only when you're sick. "It's for my mental health" doesn't count. Integrity in your personal life means being accountable to your loved ones at all times, never lying or misrepresenting anything to them. It means understanding that you are unfaithful when you make sarcastic comments about your husband to your best friend or when you fail to defend him when someone else makes a sarcastic comment about him.

Integrity also means being honest with yourself, accepting that you have failings and understanding what they are, while planning to improve them. If you think you're already perfect, it can be hard to grow and learn.

Perseverance

Perseverance, the unwillingness to give up, even if a task appears too difficult to do, yields substantial rewards. Many Tae Kwon Do techniques seem difficult, if not impossible, at first. Mastery requires perseverance. If a technique seems difficult, you shouldn't simply abandon it and move on to the next one. Perseverance means working on a particular technique until you can do the technique as it was intended. Sometimes this can take weeks, months, even years but you must not let frustration convince you to give up.

Perseverance helps you meet your martial arts goals, and it helps you shape them. Through perseverance you may learn, for instance, that you can do a jump reverse kick after all. And if you can do a jump reverse kick, well, then, you can do any jump kick. Thus, a whole group of otherwise unattainable goals can suddenly open up for you, and you can achieve them.

Practicing perseverance in the training hall prepares you for many of the challenges you face in life. For example, perhaps your work situation is frustrating. Perseverance means you try to solve the problem. Instead of finding a new job, however, this may take the form of transferring to a different department, or talking with your boss to develop a way to make your work life more bearable. Perseverance doesn't mean you stick with the same thing when it doesn't work. It sometimes means finding a different method for achieving what you want to achieve. Perseverance pays off in reaching personal or career goals and dreams.

Self-Control

Self-control refers to both the control of your body and the control of your emotions. It requires that you use wisdom and judgement to restrain your physical and mental reactions. Too often, we make decisions or react according to fear and anger. That's no way to live. Self-control, which is simply a matter of discipline, leads to a healthier, happier life.

In the training hall, self-control is a matter of controlling your physical body. For example, when you spar someone, you don't need to hit her hard enough to knock her down. You demonstrate control by sparring so that you can always adjust your power and speed. One partner may not mind your hitting her hard while another finds such physical contact frightening or unpleasant. It is your responsibility to learn this about others and to control your body enough that the martial arts experience can be a good one for everyone.

Self-control also means using your willpower to stay fit, so that you will perform at your peak level. This means you sometimes have to forgo a night on the town or substitute salad for your favorite french fries.

Controlling your emotions helps you succeed in the training hall. If you can control feelings of frustration and disappointment, you'll have more success in your training. For example, if you're learning a new form and it's more difficult for you than usual, don't allow your frustration to interfere with your ability to learn. If you start focusing on your frustration, then you allow doubt and fear to creep in, which means the process of learning your form will take even longer — and will become an even more unpleasant experience as well! If needed, step back from whatever is causing your lack of control, and take a moment to re-focus on the task at hand. Committing yourself to learning the form without getting frustrated by it shows your self-control.

When working with others, self-control means restricting how you express your feelings. If your partner is taking a long time to learn something, she isn't helped if you express this opinion. Self-control requires that you spend a lot of time keeping your mouth shut.

Self-control has an element of respect to it, just as courtesy does. It is out of respect for your partners that you use self-control. After all, if you run out of respect for your partners and don't exercise self-control, soon you'll have no partners to work with.

Self-control outside the training hall means keeping focused on your goals, whether they're personal or work goals. If your goal is to have a happy marriage, then you will need to exercise self-control when your husband sits down to watch television for the ninth night in a row while you clean the kitchen and put the kids to bed. This does not mean he's allowed to get away with such behavior, but it means instead of screaming at him, or making pointed remarks about him, or talking about him behind his back to the kids, you simply point out, in your normal conversational tones, that you require his assistance tonight. Throwing things at him may feel better momentarily, but it does not further your goal of remaining happily married.

Self-control is a matter of restraining your first instincts and using reason and judgement to respond to your environment and to those around you.

Indomitable Spirit

At first glance, indomitable spirit seems to be the same thing as perseverance. But while they are similar in some respects, they are actually quite different qualities that you cultivate in different ways.

Perseverance means persisting, continuing to do something even when you aren't successful the first 10 times you try. Indomitable spirit, on the other hand, is having the right attitude while you embark on your 11th try. Having a positive, cheerful outlook whether you win or lose helps get you through the tough times that inevitably result during Tae Kwon Do training — and in life itself. It keeps you upbeat, focused and undiscouraged even if you don't win. It is the realization that participating in Tae Kwon Do (and life) isn't about who walks away with the gold medal, but about how you prepare and learn. If you have indomitable spirit, you cannot be beaten even if you lose a match or do poorly in a competition. The fact that you participated in the match in the first place says more about you than winning or losing does.

Indomitable spirit helps you to remain optimistic outside the training hall as well. Instead of approaching life in the cynical, pessimistic way that is currently fashionable, it means remaining positive that you'll find solutions to your problems, and that no matter what difficulties come your way, you'll be equipped to handle them. Indomitable spirit makes handling all the challenges of daily life a little easier to take.

Indomitable spirit makes you a good role model for others. It can be inspirational for others to see that even if life throws us some unexpected difficulties, we nonetheless manage to keep focused on our goals and remain positive about our experiences.

Following the Tenets

Following the Five Tenets of Tae Kwon Do requires a consistent, dedicated effort. But doing so makes you a better person as well as a better martial artist. Many Tae Kwon Do practitioners keep a list of the Five Tenets where they will see it at home and at work, to help remind them of the qualities they strive to achieve. Practicing the Five Tenets helps you create balance and harmony in your life, which leads to a more satisfying, rewarding life.

DEVELOPING CHI

The right practice of Tae Kwon Do develops your chi, or inner energy. Tapping your chi (sometimes spelled "ki" or "qi"), makes you a more powerful martial artist and indeed a more powerful person.

Martial artists disagree on what exactly chi is and whether it even exists. Most feel that some form of inner energy develops through martial arts practice, and what we call it doesn't matter. Some martial artists believe chi is a life force that can be controlled and directed at opponents (think Luke Skywalker, the Force, Jedi Knights). To these martial artists, chi is a mystical force that you can learn to manipulate. Others think of chi as simply the ability to focus your energy on a specific goal. The yell ("kihop" in Korean) that you hear martial artists use helps them focus as they perform a difficult task. This yell comes from the abdomen where the chi exists. Breathing exercises can be used to develop both the chi and the kihop. These breathing exercises relieve stress and calm you down.

Correctly using your chi improves your power, focus and determination. By practicing your Tae Kwon Do techniques repeatedly and by concentrating only on what you're doing in the moment, you can tap into your chi.

MARTIAL ARTS MINDSETS

When you train in Tae Kwon Do, you need to develop certain martial arts mindsets in order to succeed. These mindsets only come with practice.

The first is the ability to remain calm and detached even when confronted by a threat or difficulty. The cultivation of this mindset is why so many exercises in Tae Kwon Do are done under controlled circumstances. By learning to perform actions without worrying about unnecessary details, you learn to confront challenges without worrying about your response. Instead, you'll feel calm and detached, confident that you'll reach an appropriate solution to the problem. Self-control is essential to developing this mindset.

In addition, you must develop the skill of intense focus. This means concentrating on what is most important at the moment. If you can develop this skill, you'll remain alert and ready. If you're alert and ready, you won't be surprised, indecisive and fearful. (It should go without saying that you're unlikely to make wise choices if you're surprised, indecisive and fearful.) Some advanced martial artists can tell whether another person has cultivated intense focus merely by looking at him or her. The state of concentration and alertness is that obvious to them. Remaining calm and detached while at the same time intensely focused helps you pass tests of all kinds — not just martial arts or physical tests, but emotional and mental tests. The physical practice of Tae Kwon Do helps you achieve these mental mindsets.

But such skills are worthless without heart. You can have great martial art talent, but without heart, you will ultimately fail. A martial artist without heart is not a martial artist at all. A person with heart can easily defeat a person with greater skill but no heart. Heart is the emotional dedication and commitment to Tae Kwon Do. It comes from doing your best at all times. It is the result of faithfully practicing the techniques of Tae Kwon Do and from living according to the Five Tenets.

Um-Yang

The well-known concept of yin-yang ("um-yang" in Korean) refers to balance. Um-yang describes how the universe works. Everything consists of opposing yet harmonious elements that depend on each other for their meaning. There can be no night without day, no warmth without cold. You can achieve balance only through understanding this relationship of opposites.

Um means the destructive elements in the universe and is associated with the passive, feminine aspects of the universe. *Yang* means the constructive (creative) elements in the universe and is associated with the active, masculine aspects of the universe. These opposites combine to create a whole. To become the best martial artist possible, you must combine the hard and the soft, the passive and the active, the masculine and the feminine.

Practicing um-yang means never going to one extreme or another but instead attempting to find balance between extremes, and to exercise moderation in all things.

Meditation

When you have doubt, fear and confusion, you're more likely to fail. These problems usually stem from your own attitude. Through commitment to the practice of Tae Kwon Do, you can eliminate these harmful emotions and encourage postive, constructive beliefs and attitudes.

You can develop mental clarity through meditation techniques. These techniques can be used to focus your thoughts, visualize self-improvement and success, and reflect on spiritual or religious issues.

Tae Kwon Do practitioners frequently use a form of meditation to achieve a calm and detached mind. The goal is to control and stop all thoughts in order to attain an empty, harmonious mind. You can go a step further and practice visualization, in which you empty your mind and then consider the aspects of your martial arts performance that you would like to improve. By visualizing the improvement you desire, you're more likely to achieve it. These types of meditation are not the same as meditation that leads to enlightenment, which is attempted in Zen Buddhism.

Chi and Breathing

Tae Kwon Do practitioners use breathing exercises to tap into their chi, which helps them relax enough to meditate and to improve their focus. The basic technique is to breathe slowly and deeply through the nose, then exhale slowly through the mouth.

When you practice this slow breathing, your breath should go deep into your stomach, and your chest and abdomen should visibly move in and out. You can use this basic slow-breathing technique after a workout to recover from exertion and at intervals throughout a workout to make sure you're getting enough oxygen. This simple exercise can quickly improve your stamina and endurance.

Focused breathing can help you relax in order to meditate or to concentrate your attention on a difficult task at hand. In this case, you deliberately slow your breath rate, which helps you calm down. When you're stressed, you tend to breathe quick, shallow breaths, which can make you feel light-headed and distracted. Instead, focus on breathing in through the nose and out through the mouth. As you breathe, take a few seconds longer with each breath, gradually lengthening the time between breaths until you're relaxed and breathing normally, slowly and without effort.

Always be aware of your breathing. Never hold your breath when you're performing the techniques. This decreases the oxygen to the brain and to the muscles, which, of course, makes physical exertion more difficult. When you practice physical techniques, exhale as you strike out with the technique (that is, when you exert yourself). Then breathe in as you return to the starting position. As you concentrate on your breathing, you'll notice improved endurance and better techniques.

Chi Creates a Strong Kihop

You have to yell (kihop) when you perform certain techniques. The kihop helps you focus your energy. In some cases, you use a kihop to let your partner know you're ready to begin working. You don't use a word when you kihop, although some people yell "hye" because it requires an abdominal contraction (where the chi is located) to yell that specific sound.

You don't need to kihop every time you perform a technique, but it is important to learn how. Women sometimes feel self-conscious when they yell, so they tend to downplay the kihop. But this is self-defeating. The less you use the kihop, the less comfortable you become with it. Instead, practice your kihop, even if you have to do it while you're alone. Try using a kihop for the first five techniques of your workout or after every third technique. The point is that without practice, you'll never develop a strong kihop.

Experiment with different yells until you find one that you're comfortable with. A good kihop shouldn't be high-pitched. It shouldn't be a shriek or a scream. It should come from your solar plexus (the abdomen). To locate your solar plexus, exhale slowly. With three fingers, press against your abdomen a few inches above your navel. When you press, you should feel the difference in your breathing. Concentrate on that point in your abdomen when you shout.

By finding and using your chi and cultivating an appropriate martial arts mindset, you will develop intense focus and winning spirit, two qualities that will make you a stronger, more successful martial artist — and a stronger, more successful person.

PART TWO:
PRACTICING TAE KWON DO:
BEGINNER

4
WHERE TO BEGIN

WHAT TO WEAR

Martial artists usually work out in a uniform (called a "dobok" in Korean). This consists of a pair of loose-fitting trousers and a loose-fitting top secured with a rank belt. Rarely do Tae Kwon Do students wear shoes. Working barefoot conditions your feet to withstand the physical stress of kicking and performing footwork. Also, you may find it difficult to learn to pivot and turn while wearing shoes. Once you understand the basics of Tae Kwon Do, you should occasionally practice the techniques in shoes, even in street clothes, so that you'll be prepared should you need to use your Tae Kwon Do techniques for self-defense. Of course, shoes should always be worn if you're working out on an uneven or hard surface. In that case, invest in specially-designed martial arts shoes. These lightweight shoes have a built-in pivot point at the ball of the foot.

You don't need to wear a uniform when you're working out on your own, but some people always do because they feel that putting the uniform on reminds them to treat the martial art with respect and to work as hard as possible. If you decide to wear regular workout clothes, choose comfortable sweatpants and a T-shirt. Don't wear anything tight or binding. Tuck your shirt tails in so your shirt won't get caught and tear.

Never wear jewelry of any kind; even your engagement or wedding ring should come off. It is easy to snag your jewelry and damage it (or you) as you're kicking and punching. And if you're working with a partner, your jewelry is dangerous to him or her as well.

You should wear contact lenses instead of glasses, or else invest in specially-designed sports glasses. If you work with a partner, she'll be kicking to your head, and your glasses must withstand a stray hit.

Don't wear cosmetics. It can run, stain your clothes and get in your eyes. Keep your nails trimmed short so that they don't snag something (including your partner). Besides, it's difficult to make a fist with two-inch nails.

PRACTICE AREA

When you practice on your own, you'll need an open space to work out. Try to clear an area at least 8 feet by 8 feet to practice your techniques, forms and sparring. Some people use the basement, garage or backyard. If you can, however, work out on a carpeted floor, because your bare feet move and pivot more easily. Working out on a concrete floor, such as you find in the garage or basement, can be very hard on your joints. Try to find an alternative or at the least put down a square of padded carpet on top of the concrete.

EQUIPMENT YOU'LL NEED

The essential equipment you need to practice Tae Kwon Do is yourself, some workout clothes and instructions (such as this book). But there are certain other pieces of equipment that can help you get the most from your training. Invest in a uniform and martial arts shoes first. Uniforms cost between $35 and $100, depending on the weight and type of material used. Shoes cost about $50 or $60.

For practicing your techniques and your sparring, a heavy bag makes an excellent substitute for a partner. Two different kinds of heavy bags are available: hanging and freestanding. Hanging heavy bags attach to a ceiling joist. They have the greatest range of motion and are most like sparring a person. But if you're renting, don't want a heavy bag hanging in your living room, or object for another reason, a freestanding heavy bag can be used. These have a base filled with water or sand to keep them from tipping over. They can easily be moved out of the way. If you have $100 and nothing better to spend it on, think about investing in a heavy bag.

If possible, place a full-length mirror where you can see your reflection as you work out. This helps you keep your body in the correct position. A video camera can show you what you really look like as you perform Tae Kwon Do techniques.

Target bags and focus mitts help you learn to kick and punch correctly and powerfully, but require a partner to use. So unless you have someone who will hold them for you, a heavy bag is a better investment.

If you're sparring with partners, purchase sparring equipment, which will help protect you and your partners from injury. A set of sparring gear can run between $100 and $200, depending on what you purchase. Most Tae Kwon Do practitioners use foot pads and hand pads; some use headgear. Shin guards and forearm guards help prevent bruises, so they can be a good addition if you're susceptible. A chest protector can keep your ribs safe.

If you plan to practice takedowns, or if you're sparring on a hard floor, consider purchasing a mat, which can be had for less than $100. See Part 9, Chapter 5, for information on finding martial arts equipment.

WORKOUT GUIDELINES

Practice some of your techniques every day, to keep them fresh in your mind, especially new techniques or ones that you're having difficulty mastering. You can also stretch off and on throughout the day.

For full-fledged workouts, every other day is adequate. You can work out more often, but you don't want to overdo it and risk injury. Also, you may want to devote some time to weight training or aerobic training in order to improve your martial arts performance, and these may be difficult to fit in if you're doing a full-fledged Tae Kwon Do workout every day. Of course, some people find that they don't need or want to do other workouts, and so practicing Tae Kwon Do every day suits their needs perfectly.

Beginners often work out too enthusiastically at first, then find that they're suffering muscle strains and soreness and that they've burned out. It's always a good idea to temper your enthusiasm until you and your body are accustomed to the workout you'll be going through.

A full-fledged workout consists of warming up, stretching, techniques practice, forms practice, self-defense practice, sparring practice and cooling down. An hour is a good length of time to practice, because you can work up a good sweat without having to commit half your day to it.

SAMPLE WORKOUT

Warm up and stretching (10 minutes)
Practice techniques (15 minutes)
Self-defense practice (10 minutes)
Forms practice (10 minutes)
Step sparring and free sparring (15 minutes)

As you learn more forms, you'll spend more time on forms practice and less time on techniques practice. Allot a specific amount of time to each part so that nothing gets shortchanged. Keep a clock in your workout area. Limiting the amount of time you spend on any one part will prevent boredom and loss of interest during practice. You'll always have plenty of variety by adding in new techniques and drills.

5
WARM-UPS AND STRETCHES

WARMING UP

The first step in your Tae Kwon Do workout is to warm up. Beginning martial artists often complain of muscle soreness, and even strains and tears. Many – perhaps all – of these problems can be prevented with proper preparation.

Start with a simple warm-up method, such as a brisk walk or jog. Some people like to jump rope or stairwalk. Warm up for a few minutes until you feel loose, start sweating lightly and notice faster breathing. Then you can begin stretching in preparation for a more vigorous workout.

Stretching

You should stretch before you begin any workout, but it is especially important for Tae Kwon Do practitioners because of all the high kicks and other difficult techniques. Stretching helps you increase your flexibility over time, and it helps you prepare for your workout so that you don't strain your muscles when you try to kick higher. Tight, rigid muscles are more prone to tears, sprains and strains. Loose, warmed-up muscles stretch instead of tear.

For each stretch, hold the stretched position for 10 to 30 seconds. Don't bounce, but move smoothly from the starting position to the stretched position. You should be able to feel the stretch, but you shouldn't feel pain. (If you do feel pain, stop and relax! If the pain persists, check with your healthcare provider.) Give yourself plenty of time to go through all of your stretches, and feel free to add or try different stretches as you learn them.

Figure 1

Neck Stretch

To stretch your neck, don't rotate your head in all directions, which can pinch a nerve. Instead, stretch your neck in each of the four directions. Tuck your chin to your chest. Hold for 10 seconds. Then, tilt your head to the left, trying to touch your shoulder. Again, hold for 10 seconds. Next, tilt your head to the right, trying to touch your shoulder. Hold. Finally, lean your head to the back. Look up at the ceiling and tilt your head as far back as you can. Hold. Repeat two or three times, until your neck feels loose and limber (see figure 1).

Shoulder Stretch

Extend your arm parallel to the floor. Bring it across your chest, without bending your elbow. You should feel the stretch in the back of your shoulder and in the upper arm area. Use your other hand to hold your arm in place. Hold the stretch for 10 seconds. Keeping your arm extended, reach to the back. Don't twist. Simply reach as far behind you as you can. Hold for 10 seconds. Relax and repeat five times for each shoulder (see figure 2).

Figure 2

Figure 3

Arm Rotation

Extend both arms parallel to the floor. Make circles with your arms, going forward, then backward. Work slowly, stretching the muscles, not bouncing them. Spend 15 seconds moving your arms in each direction, then relax and repeat (see figure 3).

Wrist Stretch

Extend your arm slightly. Open your hand so that your palm is flat. With your other hand, gently pull your fingers back. Hold for 10 seconds. Then press your fingers forward. Hold for 10 seconds. Repeat three or four times for each hand (see figure 4).

Figure 4

Figure 5

Back Stretch

Sit on the floor with your legs crossed. Keeping your back straight, bend forward at the waist. Try to touch your chin or your chest to your legs. Don't bounce. Once you've stretched as far forward as you can, hold the position for 10 seconds. Then relax and repeat five times.

To get a better stretch, put your arms out in front of you as far as possible. Touch the ground in front of your legs with your palms down flat. Then try to lower your elbows to the ground. This helps you stretch your back farther (see figure 5).

Figure 6

Hip Stretch

To stretch the muscles that extend from your hip to the top of your thigh, kneel with one knee on the floor. Bend the other knee at a 90-degree angle, with your foot flat on the floor. Keeping your upper body straight, slowly roll your hips forward until you can feel the stretch on the top of your hip and thigh. Support yourself, if necessary, by placing your hands on the floor. Hold the forward position for 10 seconds, then relax, return to the starting position and repeat. Switch legs and repeat (see figure 6).

Open Stretch

To stretch the groin area and the lower back, sit with your legs spread in a V-shape. Keep them as far apart as possible. Bending at the waist, lean toward your left leg, as if you were trying to touch your chest to your left knee. Reach for your left foot. Try to touch the bottom of your left foot with both hands. Keep your back straight and don't bend your knees. Hold the

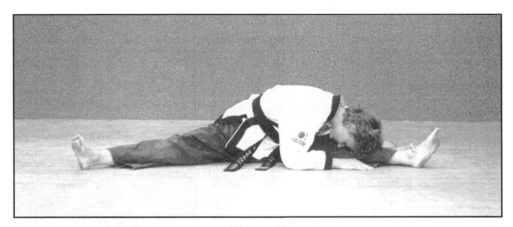

Figure 7

Figure 8

position for 10 seconds, then relax. Reach toward the right side and hold the stretch for 10 seconds, then relax. Finally, lean forward between your legs, as if you were trying to touch your chest to the ground between your legs. Hold the position for 10 seconds (see figures 7 and 8).

Figure 9

Variation:

To stretch your groin area farther, return to an upright position, your legs still in the V-shape. Pull your feet toward you until the soles of your feet are touching each other. Continue moving your legs toward you as far as you can. Hold the position for 10 seconds. Then, lean forward and try to touch your chin to your legs. Hold the position for 10 seconds. Relax and repeat (see figure 9).

Figure 10

Figure 11

Hamstring Stretch

On your back, extend your legs straight out in front of you. Place your hands under your lower back for support if you need it. Lift one leg up and extend it at a 90-degree angle to the floor. Keeping your knee straight, try to touch your knee to your shoulder. For an additional stretch, slip a towel around your calf and pull the ends of the towel toward you, pulling your leg forward. Don't overdo the stretch and don't bounce. Hold for 10 seconds, then relax and repeat. Lower your leg to the floor and stretch the other leg (see figure 10).

Variation:

Pull one knee toward your chest until you feel the stretch. Hold 10 seconds. Repeat five times with each leg (see figure 11).

Figure 12

Quadriceps Stretch

Use a wall for support. Extend your leg out behind you and bend your knee. With one hand, reach behind you and pull your foot toward your buttocks. Lift so that you feel the stretch in the quadriceps muscle (the front of the thigh). Hold for 10 seconds. Repeat five times for each leg (see figure 12).

Calf Stretch

Standing upright, lift your heels off the ground until you are standing on your toes. Use a wall for support if you need. Hold this stretch for 10 seconds, then relax and repeat five times. Next, lower your heels to the ground and tilt back until your toes are off the ground. Hold. Repeat five times (see figures 13 and 14).

Figure 13   **Figure 14**

Figure 15

Ankle Rotation

Sit on the floor with one leg crossed over the other. Lift your top foot slightly, and rotate it in a circular motion, moving it in all directions. Use your hands to help stretch. Do several rotations with each ankle. Start slowly and gradually increase speed as you repeat the stretch (see figure 15).

Cooling Down

After you've completed your workout, don't skip cooling down. If you've been working out vigorously and then just stop, you're setting yourself up for sore muscles and perhaps overuse injuries. Take five minutes or so to cool down. Your cool down can be the same as your warm-up. For instance, you can jog, starting quickly and then slowing down, or you can walk, at first briskly and then more slowly. Some martial artists cool down by performing their techniques slowly and gently during the cool-down period. Some people prefer to end with a few simple stretches, much as they began their workout with. The above stretches can be done after warming up and/or as part of the cool-down period.

6
BEGINNER STANCES

Your body position when you perform a technique is called a stance. The placement of your feet and the line of your body provides balance for attacks or defense. Although almost any technique can be performed in any stance, different stances have different advantages and drawbacks. For example, the front stance is a very solid stance. You're unlikely to get knocked over if you're in a good front stance. However, in the front stance, your body is more open and unguarded, leaving you vulnerable to attack. On the other hand, the back stance allows you to keep your body better guarded, but it is not as solid of a stance.

Therefore, practice all of the techniques you learn using the different stances so that you can understand the benefits and drawbacks of each.

READY STANCE

The first stance you learn, the ready stance (see figure 16), is the position you take to focus yourself before you begin your workout. It is also the stance you take before you begin a form. The Korean term for "ready" is "chunbee," so this stance is sometimes called the chunbee stance.

Stand up straight with your feet comfortably apart. Bend your elbows at a 45-degree angle and make your hands into fists. Hold

Figure 16

your arms in front of and slightly away from your body. Look directly in front of you. Focus on the activity you're about to perform, and don't allow yourself to become distracted.

ATTENTION STANCE

The attention stance is used to show respect for others (see figure 17). You come to attention when an instructor or senior student approaches you. The Korean word for "attention" is "chareyhet," so this is sometimes called the chareyhet stance.

Stand up straight with your feet together. The inner edges of your feet should touch. Hold your arms straight at your sides, slightly away from your body. Make your hands into

Figure 17

fists (some instructors prefer palms open.) Look directly in front of you. You should never look around; this is considered disrespectful. Nothing should distract you from the attention stance.

Once you have paid your respects to your instructor, you will generally be told to assume the ready stance.

Figure 18

HORSE STANCE

The horse stance is also called the horseback stance or the riding horse stance. Stand with your feet about a shoulder and a half's width apart, your feet parallel to each other. Bend your knees to a 90-degree angle. Hold your arms, hands as fists, in front of your chest to protect it (see figure 18).

FRONT STANCE

Tae Kwon Do practitioners use the front stance (sometimes called the forward stance) quite frequently. Stand with your feet about a shoulder's width apart. Step forward with one leg, bending it at a 90-degree angle. Slide the other leg back so that your leg is straight behind you. Don't bend your knee. Keep the soles of both feet on the floor. (This requires flexibility and may require some work at first.) Bend your elbows and make your hands into fists. Your chest and hips should both be facing forward.

The front stance can be lengthened by stepping farther forward, or it can be shortened by bringing the forward leg back slightly and decreasing the angle of the bend. The long front stance is used for thrusting strikes and the short stance is used for overhead strikes. The normal front stance can be used for most other techniques (see figure 19).

BACK STANCE

The back stance presents a smaller target to your opponent. Although you look to the front, your chest and hips face the side. Stand with your chest and hips facing the side and your head turned to face the front. Place your feet so that your front foot points in the same direction you are looking. Your back foot should be perpendicular to your front foot. Your forward foot should rest slightly in front

Figure 19

of you. Bend your back knee to a 90-degree angle and shift your body so that 80% of your weight rests on your back leg. This allows you to strike quickly with your front leg. Keep your back hand forward so that it guards your chest. Your forward arm should be bent at the elbow, ready to block or strike at anything that comes to the front (see figure 20).

FIGHTING STANCE

The fighting stance (see figure 21), a variation of the back stance, is used during sparring. Keep your feet the same as in the back stance, but distribute your weight evenly so you can use your front leg and your back leg equally. In the fighting stance, your head and chest face slightly forward while your hips

Figure 20

Figure 21

remain facing the side. With your chest forward, you can strike quickly with either hand. Make your hands into fists and hold them in front of your hands in a guarded positions, ready to strike.

STANCE BASICS

Most Tae Kwon Do techniques are performed from the front stance or the back stance. When used in sparring, most techniques are performed in the fighting stance. Kicks that use the the forward leg are done slightly differently from kicks that use the rear leg.

The lower you keep your body, the stronger the stance. Practice stances so that you can hold a stance position for a long period of time with your knees bent as much as possible. When you perform techniques or spar, you may not need or want to stay in a deep "strong" stance, but you must acquire the ability to do so. Strong stances help your balance and develop your leg strength. Since Tae Kwon Do relies so much on kicking, it is essential to build this strength and endurance.

Use stance stretches to increase your flexibility. Position yourself in any of the stances described above, then lower the stance until you feel the stretch. Hold for about 10 seconds, then repeat. You can build strength by holding the low stretches for a minute or two at a time. As you develop strength, you can hold the position for five or 10 minutes at a time. This makes for very strong quadriceps muscles, which are essential to high kicking.

7

BEGINNER BLOCKS

The basic defensive technique in Tae Kwon Do is the block. A block keeps an opponent's strike from landing on a vulnerable part of your body. You must perform a block quickly and sharply, because the momentum helps you defend against the attack. A block should be just as powerful as a kick or punch. In most cases, you block with the inner part of your forearm, which is the most muscular and well-protected part of your arm. Most blocks have a twisting movement at the end, which helps deflect the attack.

By using a stronger part of your body to defend a weaker part, you're less likely to sustain an injury during an attack. In addition, blocked kicks and punches don't count in sparring matches.

Different blocks protect different parts of your body. The low block protects your legs, especially your knees, and the groin area. Middle blocks (such as crescent blocks) protect your midsection, such as your ribs. High blocks protect your head, neck and shoulders.

LOW BLOCK

The low block protects your knee and leg. Stand in a front stance. With your forward arm (on the same side as your forward leg), make a fist. Bring your fist up to the opposite shoulder. Your palm faces upward. Sweep your arm down across your body, stopping slightly beyond your knee. At the end of the block, twist your wrist so that your palm faces down. The block and twist should be done in one motion, but don't twist too soon or you'll lose the power of the twist. Block with the inner surface of your arm. Keep your wrist and hand strong, so that you can easily push a kick or punch away (see figures 22

Figure 22

Figure 23

and 23).

HIGH BLOCK

Stand in a front stance. Make both hands into fists and place both hands slightly in front of your body. Your forward arm will perform the block. Bend this arm, placing your fist under your opposite arm near the shoulder. Keep your palm up.

Pull your opposite arm back toward your side, keeping your hand in a fist. As you do so, sweep your blocking arm up, keeping your elbow cocked at a 45-degree angle. The block should stop slightly above the top of your head. At the end of the block, twist your wrist so that the palm of your hand faces the ceiling. You should be able to see under your raised blocking arm, and it should

Figure 24

Figure 25

Figure 26

Figure 27

protect the top of your head from a downward strike (see figures 24 and 25).

CRESCENT BLOCKS

Crescent blocks protect the middle section of your body from an attack. Like the low block and the high block, you perform them with a sweeping motion and a twist of the wrist. There are two different crescent blocks, one that sweeps to the outside and one that sweeps to the inside. Generally, you block to the outside if someone attacks with a weapon or a thrusting technique. This way, you won't deflect the weapon into your chest. You block to the inside when your opponent is punching or kicking and you want to protect yourself without exposing your chest to a secondary attack.

Inside-to-Outside Crescent Block

In a fighting stance, cock both elbows and make both hands into fists. Your forward arm is your blocking arm. Begin by placing your blocking hand under your opposite arm (as you do with a high block). Your palm should face down with your arm parallel to the floor. Sweep your blocking arm forward so that it moves toward your forward leg. As you sweep, raise your forearm so that it becomes perpendicular to the ground. The block should stop just beyond your forward leg. As you finish the block, twist your wrist so that your palm faces you. Bend your blocking arm to slightly less than a 90 degree angle.

As you perform the block, pull your opposite, non-blocking arm back to your side. Keep your elbow cocked and your hand in a fist, ready to strike or block again as needed. At all times, keep your chest turned away from the attacker (see figures 26 and 27).

Outside-to-Inside Crescent Block

In a fighting stance, make both hands into fists. With your forward hand, which will perform the block, reach back behind you, twisting at the waist.

Figure 28　　　　　　　　**Figure 29**

Cock your elbow at a 90-degree angle and keep your upper arm parallel to the floor, palm facing away from you. Sweep your blocking arm forward from back to front. Untwist at the waist as you block. Your block should end just past your leg. As you finish the block, twist your wrist so that your palm faces you.

As you perform the block, pull your opposite, non-blocking hand back to your side. Keep the elbow cocked and keep your hand in a fist, ready to react. Again, keep your chest turned away from the attacker at all times (see figures 28 and 29).

SINGLE KNIFE HAND BLOCK

The knife hand block also protects your midsection. You perform it in almost the same way you perform an inside-to-outside crescent block, except

Figure 30　　　　　　　　**Figure 31**

your hand is in the knife hand position. Again, assume a back stance position. Your forward arm is your blocking arm. Make your blocking hand into a knife hand. To do this, flatten your fingers and keep your hand rigid and your muscles tight. Bend your thumb at the knuckle and keep it tight against your hand. Make your back, non-blocking hand into a fist. Your non-blocking arm should guard your chest.

Begin the block by placing your blocking hand palm up above your opposite shoulder. Sweep your arm across your body. Keep your elbow cocked at a 90-degree angle. Stop your block when it goes just past your forward leg. As you finish the block, twist your wrist so that the outer edge of your hand blocks the attack. Your palm should face away from you. As you perform the block, pull your non-blocking hand back to your side, keeping your elbow cocked and your hand a fist, ready to block or strike as needed (see figures 30 and 31).

DOUBLE KNIFE HAND BLOCKS

These blocks are a variation of the single knife hand block. While the single knife hand block is faster, the double knife hand block uses both hands to block an attack, so it is more powerful. A double knife hand block can protect the middle section or the low section. You use a different technique depending on the section you're blocking.

Double Knife Hand Block, Middle Section

This technique can be done from any stance, but to learn it, use the back stance. Start with both hands in a knife hand position. This means your hands should be straight, your fingers rigid and held tightly together, and your thumb bent slightly at the middle knuckle. Reach behind you. Your back arm should extend straight back, palm facing down. Your forward arm should extend across your chest, palm facing up.

Sweep your arms quickly across your body. As you block, both elbows

Figure 32   Figure 33

should be cocked at a 90-degree angle. Twist your wrists so that the palm of your forward hand faces out and the palm of your back hand faces up. Your forward arm stops in a position just above your forward leg, and your back arm covers your midsection, slightly away from your body (see figures 32 and 33).

Double Knife Hand Block, Low Section

This technique is similar to the double knife hand block, middle section.

Figure 34

There are a few minor changes. Instead of reaching straight behind you, reach up toward the ceiling or the sky. Hold your hands so that the palm of your forward hand faces up and the palm of your back hand faces down. Sweep down across your body. Stop your forward arm, fingers pointing toward the ground, when it is parallel to your front leg. Keep your arm straight, about 8 to 10 inches in front of your leg and turn your palm so that it faces inward, toward your knee. At the same time, block downward with your back hand until it reaches your midsection. Cock your elbow at a 90-degree angle and twist your hand so that your palm faces up (see figure 34).

8

BEGINNER HAND STRIKING TECHNIQUES

Once you've learned the basic blocks, you're ready to work on striking or attacking techniques — kicks, punches, and those hand techniques we used to call "karate chops" when we were kids.

Beginners typically learn just a few basic kicks and a few basic hand techniques. These form a foundation on which you can build, so you must master these basics, even if it means repeating them dozens (even hundreds) of times a day. Such practice leads to "muscle memory," training that results in your being able to perform a technique without even thinking about it. At first, however, you will think about your techniques a lot — maybe too much. This is OK. Just remember that you're a beginner, and don't be too hard on yourself if the techniques don't seem to come as easily as you think they should.

VARIETIES OF HAND STRIKING TECHNIQUES

There are many different ways to use your hands in order to strike, and this book will show you most of them. However, the basic punch is the most important one to learn. Hand striking techniques include all of the techniques that use any part of the hand to strike. This includes the palm, the back of the fist, and both edges of the hand.

PURPOSE OF HAND TECHNIQUES

Because women have less powerful upper bodies than men, they tend to rely on other techniques, such as kicks, when they're sparring and practicing their martial arts techniques. But having strong punches gives a woman many advantages. In sparring, punches and other hand techniques are used in close range. Most female martial artists learn that this is their best tactic, since when they spar men (and most female martial artists do), men often have the advantage in kicking range because they frequently have longer legs.

Hand techniques are also useful in self-defense where you may be seated or prone when attacked and not in position to use your legs. (See Part 6, Chapters 22 through 25 for more details.)

PRACTICE OF HAND TECHNIQUES

New martial artists often favor one hand or one leg. If a person is right handed, for instance, she'll practice her techniques using only her right hand. Practicing this way causes a lack of balance. Excellent martial artists can use both hands and both feet to strike, with equal skill. This should be your goal. On a practical level, such balance helps you in situations where you might be caught off-guard. For example: you're getting into your car and someone grabs you from behind. Only your left leg is free and unobstructed. If you've been practicing techniques equally on both right and left legs, you can easily kick the attacker, giving yourself enough time to either get in the car and slam the door or assume a fighting position. Or, suppose you've broken your right arm roller-blading. Some criminals look for weak victims, and someone with a broken arm is a perfect candidate. However, if you've been practicing your techniques using both arms and legs equally, you'll be able to strike at the attacker with your left hand and land just as powerful a blow as you might have done with your right.

To sum up, always practice each technique for the same number of repetitions on each side. If you come across a technique you find particularly difficult to do on one side, increase the number of repetitions you do on that side until you're comfortable with your skill level, and then go back to practicing equally.

STRAIGHT PUNCH

The first attacking technique you learn is the straight punch. Although it can be performed in any stance, it is easiest to learn in a front stance. Assume a front stance. Your forward hand will perform the punch.

Make your hand into a fist. To do so, roll your fingers into a ball and fold your thumb over to lock your fingers in place. You should feel a light amount of tension in your forearm when you've made a good fist. The knuckles on your first two fingers (those closest to the thumb) make up the striking area. On impact, only these two knuckles touch the target. If more of your hand touches the target, you may be rolling your wrist, making a fist incorrectly, or otherwise performing the technique wrong. Striking a target incorrectly can cause injury, so practice this technique (and all others) slowly at first, without a target, gaining momentum as you gain skill, and hitting targets (and sparring partners) only after you've learned the technique.

To perform the punch, "chamber" your arm. To "chamber" means to assume the ready position for the strike. For this technique, you chamber your arm by pulling your arm back to your side and bending your elbow at a 90-degree angle. Turn your palm so that it faces up.

Then punch straight forward with your arm, crossing slightly in front of your body so that if you look down at your extended arm, your fist will be on line with the center of your body. As you finish the punch, turn your wrist so that your palm faces down. This twisting motion adds more power to your punch. For additional power, turn your hips into the punch, keeping your feet planted firmly in your stance.

For practice, high punches strike at the height of your nose, not above your head. Middle punches strike to an area corresponding to your solar plexus. Of course, in actual use, your high punch will go as high as it needs to strike an attacker's nose or throat, and a middle punch will be the height of your attacker's midsection.

Completely extend your punching arm, but don't lock your elbow — this could cause injury on impact. Don't stop at the target but continue your punch into the target. This is known as the follow-through, and it's where you can generate additional power.

Finally, once you have executed the technique, return your hand to its starting position, chambered at your side (see figures 35 and 36).

REVERSE PUNCH

The reverse punch, a variation of the straight punch, is used more often than the straight punch because it is more powerful. You perform a reverse punch and a straight punch in exactly the same way. The only difference is in

Figure 35   **Figure 36**

Figure 37

the punching hand. The straight punch is performed using the forward hand. The reverse punch, however, is performed using the back hand.

Assume a front stance. If your left leg is forward, chamber and punch with your *right* hand. Because of the difference in foot placement and body position, you can get more of your body behind this punch, making it more powerful (see figure 37).

PRACTICING PUNCHES

Performing punching techniques correctly depends on hand position as well as hand movement. Keep your wrist straight so that the back of your fist and your knuckles are on the same plane as your forearm. Be especially certain that your knuckles don't tilt upward, a common beginner's mistake. Don't forget that starting your punch in the correct position (the chamber) and twisting your wrist at the moment of impact creates powerful, explosive punches. Practice all parts of the technique from chamber to strike to follow through to re-chamber.

Practice striking with the correct technique by reviewing the technique slowly while watching your movements in a mirror. Then lightly punch a stationary object, such as the front of a cabinet, a wall, or another hard, flat surface. Move slowly, punch lightly and pay attention to how your hand feels on impact. Does it roll forward? Does your elbow tilt up at the last minute? Is your arm completely extended? Keep working, adjusting your fist and the position of your arm and hand until you can strike with the correct part of your hand, and your punch lands and stops on impact without twisting and rolling.

Weakness in the wrist and forearm can cause twisting and rolling. If you're practicing the technique correctly, but still see problems, you may need to strengthen your wrists and forearms. In this case, use wrist wraps, available inexpensively at any sporting goods store, and work on building up these muscles. More on how to do that follows.

Using a striking post can help improve your techniques. A striking post is a type of martial arts equipment that consists of a piece of upright wood secured to the floor or the ground. Sometimes the wood is covered with carpet or other material to prevent scratches to your hands. You strike the post with your techniques to condition your hands.

ADDING POWER

In general, women have less upper body strength than men do. Because of anatomical differences, much of our strength can be found in our hips and legs. For this reason, many female martial artists favor kicking techniques. But in many circumstances relying on only one type of attack can lead to failure. No big deal if you're involved in a friendly sparring match; a much bigger deal if you're trying to fend off an attacker.

You can increase your upper body strength by lifting weights and performing conditioning exercises such as push-ups and pull-ups. These take time to work, but are well worth the effort.

To add more power immediately, perform your techniques correctly. Chamber your fist appropriately. Twist your wrist at the moment of impact to add explosive power. Make sure your whole body — not just your arm — is behind the punch, by pivoting into the punch.

Finally, you can incorporate a reciprocating motion that adds speed and power to all of your techniques, not just punches. This reciprocating motion is created by countering one movement with another. For instance, instead of just punching forward with your punching hand, you can pull back with your non-punching hand. To understand what this means, stand with your forward arm extended, as if you have just punched a target. Put your non-punching hand about 12 inches out from your midsection. With a sharp movement, pull your non-punching hand into a chambered position, fist at your waist, elbow cocked 90-degrees. As you make this movement, you should be able to feel the motion that forces your punching arm forward. Your non-punching hand, now chambered at your waist, becomes your punching hand. Your other arm, still extended, can be pulled back as you punch to generate power (see figure 38).

Figure 38

Practice this technique by standing in a front stance with both arms in front of you, elbows slightly cocked. Pull your punching arm back to its chamber position, leaving your non-punching arm forward. (It can be used to block strikes to the midsection from this position.) As you punch forward, pull your non-punching hand back to your side and chamber it. After you punch, re-chamber or pull back your punching arm to its starting position. As you do so, punch with your opposite arm. Repeat until you have the reciprocating or push-pull technique down. Always remember to use your opposite hand as a counter-balance to your striking hand in order to easily generate more power and more speed.

PALM STRIKE

The palm strike, which drives the heel of the palm into the target, can substitute for a punch. Performed in a similar fashion, you simply use a different striking surface for the palm strike. Assume a front stance. Your forward hand will actually perform the strike. Make a knife hand instead of a fist (see Knife Hand Block). Chamber your hand at your waist. Point your fingers down and turn your palm so that it faces forward. Keep your fingers tightly together. Strike forward, just as if you were punching a target. At the moment of impact, turn your wrist so that your fingers point up (see figures 39 and 40).

Just as with a punch, using reciprocating movements and putting your body behind the strike makes it more powerful.

The palm strike can be used whenever you might use a punch (except in sparring). For instance, suppose you intend to strike an attacker in the nose. Instead of a punch, you can use a palm strike, driving the heel of your hand upward. Many women prefer this technique for two reasons. First, the striking surface of a palm strike (the heel of the hand) is larger than the striking surface of a punch (the first two knuckles), so if a woman has to reach or is off-balance when she strikes, she improves her chances of successfully landing the technique. Second, because the force of the impact is spread over a wider area on her hand, she is less likely to injure herself striking. Since women tend to have smaller hands, and thus more delicate knuckles, they are more prone than men to injury when punching.

Figure 39

Figure 40

REVERSE PALM STRIKE

The reverse palm strike, like the reverse punch, is performed with the back hand rather than the forward hand. Like the reverse punch, the reverse palm strike is more powerful than the straight palm strike (see figure 41).

UPPER BODY STRENGTH

Improving your upper body strength increases the power of your hand striking techniques. If you begin these conditioning exercises soon after you start your Tae Kwon Do training, you should have built considerable strength by the time you reach the intermediate stage of Tae Kwon Do training.

Figure 41

If you have access to weight training equipment, lift weights to improve your upper body strength. Such techniques as biceps curls and triceps extensions help strengthen your arms, while butterfly presses, overhead presses, and lat pulldowns will strengthen your pectoral muscles, your shoulders, and other parts of your chest. Women can lift weights without bulking up by lifting lighter weights and doing more repetitions. Don't use weights that are too light, or you won't accomplish anything. Instead, opt for a weight that allows you to do about eight repetitions before your muscles fail and you can't lift anymore. Most personal trainers suggest doing two or three sets of eight repetitions each, with a couple minutes rest between sets. A good weight training manual will help you get started (see Lawler's *Weight Training for Martial Artists*, Turtle Press, 1999).

Although weight training certainly improves one's strength, nothing beats an old-fashioned push-up for building upper body strength. Plus you don't need special equipment and you can do them anytime.

Push-ups

Start with basic push-ups and build from there. To perform a basic push-up, rest on the floor with your palms directly under your shoulders. Feet together, place your toes on the floor so that your body weight rests on your toes and your palms. Tighten your abdomen and straighten your back and shoulders. From this position, push directly up. Fully extend your arms but don't lock your elbows out. Move smoothly and evenly. Going too fast can put too much strain on your elbows, especially in the beginning when your body may not be accustomed to the effort.

If the basic push-up position is too difficult to do at first (or your abdominal muscles need pampering, such as after childbirth or a hysterectomy), keep your knees on the floor. Although this reduces the amount of body weight

Figure 42

Figure 43

Figure 44   **Figure 45**

your arms lift and thus reduces the resistance and the effectiveness of the exercise, it does isolate the arm muscles, making them do all the work, so it serves as a reasonable substitute (see figures 42 and 43).

Start with three sets of 15 push-ups each. While your goal will change over time, aim for 75 push-ups in a row resting only on your palms and toes.

In order to strengthen different muscles in your arms and upper body, simply vary the position of your hands as you do push-ups. If you spread your hands so that your palms rest two shoulders widths apart (instead of directly under your shoulders), you will work your chest muscles more (see figure 44).

Figure 46

If you bring your hands close together under your sternum, you will work your triceps more. Be careful of this variation if you have elbow trouble, such as tendinitis (see figure 45).

Finally, if you use that old martial arts standby, the knuckle push-up, you will strengthen your wrists and forearms, leading to stronger, more correct punching techniques. You perform a knuckle push-up by resting your weight on the two punching knuckles of each fist instead of resting your weight on your open palms (see figure 46).

Pull-ups

If you have access to a pull-up bar (kits that attach to a doorway can be purchased inexpensively for home use), work on pull-ups. This is one of the most effective ways to strengthen your arms without investing in weight equipment and without spending a lot of time in the weight room. A pull-up is simple to do. Standing straight, with your feet comfortably apart, grasp the bar with your palms facing away from you, your hands in line with your shoulders. Pull yourself up from the floor. The goal is to get your chin above the bar. If you cannot do even one or two pull-ups at first, don't feel embarassed and give up – many women can't. Instead, enlist a friend to act as spotter. At a gym, you can have one of the staff members do this for you. The spotter will help you lift your weight. Some more complicated pieces of fitness equipment allow you to practice pull-ups without a spotter. Instead of lifting your entire body weight, you specify the amount of weight you will pull up and the machine does the rest.

To strengthen other muscles in your arms, change your grip on the bar. For instance, if your palms face you, you'll work your biceps more. If you grip facing away, you use more of your triceps. You can grip the bar with your hands close together or with your hands spread far apart. All of these variations increase your overall muscle strength by training and building all of the muscles in your arms and shoulders.

Your goal should be to perform pull-ups without a spotter's help. Attempt to do four sets of three. After each set of three pull-ups, vary the grip you have on the bar before going on to the next set of three. Once you can do these, add repetitions to each set of pull-ups you do. Once you can do 10 pull-ups in each of four grips, your upper body strength will be phenomenal.

9

BASIC KICKING TECHNIQUES

When you start learning kicking techniques, you begin to understand the fun — and the challenge — of Tae Kwon Do. Nothing is as exciting as learning what your body can do, and practicing kicks helps you find out about your abilities and skills.

Kicking techniques use any part of the foot as the striking surface — the ball of the foot, the top (instep) of the foot, both sides of the foot, and the heel. More powerful than hand techniques, kicks are used when the opponent is several feet away. Therefore, when an attacker or sparring partner comes toward you, a kick can stop him or her. If the kick fails to do its job, you can always follow with another kick or with a hand striking technique. This does not mean you should always choose a kick as the first weapon of attack. It depends. Sometimes an opponent manages to move in close before you can kick; in this case, you may use punches and other hand techniques. Sometimes it is wiser for you to retreat and move to kicking range.

With the exception of the crescent kicks (inside-to-outside, outside-to-inside, axe), all of the beginner kicks can be used to strike to a low, middle or high target area. The low target area is knee-level, although sometimes the groin is targeted; the middle target area includes the solar plexus and ribs; the high target area includes the shoulders, neck and head. Practice kicking to all three target areas. It requires muscle strength and flexibility to kick to the high target areas, and you may wish to add strength and flexibility training to your routine in order to enhance your skills. One of the best ways to build strength and flexibility is to repeatedly practice all of the different kicks, attempting to kick as high as you can.

You can perform the beginner kicks with either the front leg or the back leg in any stance. Front leg kicks are faster (they arrive at their target quickly) and back leg kicks are more powerful (you build momentum as you kick and can leverage your body in order to put more weight behind the kick). In sparring the front leg kick can be very effective. It can also be effective in a confrontation if you depend on it for the element of surprise, and not as a single technique that will knock the attacker out. However, in certain sparring matches where a visible shock or movement must occur for a point to count, you should rely on back leg kicks, because they're more powerful. Again, in a physical confrontation, a back leg kick (especially directed to a vulnerable area, such as a knee or groin) can be especially effective in ending the attack.

This difference has several implications for women. Women are typically faster than men for several reasons. In general, we're lighter than they are, and being lighter, can move more quickly. We also tend to be more flexible and to have less muscle mass, which means our movements are less restricted. Of course, some women are not as fast as some men, and some men are more flexible than some women, and some women have more muscle mass than some men. But you get my drift.

As you learn kicking techniques, capitalize on these tendencies. Your fast kicks can serve to distract an opponent or to score in a sparring match. Also, you can add speed to a back leg kick, which creates an advantage for you. Not only does your kick land swiftly, but it can be quite powerful. Instead of worrying about being overwhelmed by men who are bigger than you are, play to your strengths. (More information about self-defense and sparring tactics for women is offered in later chapters.)

For beginner kicks, the only difference in performing a kick using a front leg or a back leg is in how you shift your weight. For instance, in a front stance position, a front leg kick requires you to shift your weight to the back leg as you kick, whereas a back leg kick requires you to shift your weight to the front leg. Remember to practice both front and back leg kicks and to practice with both legs in both positions. For instance, practice each kick in a front stance with your left leg forward. Kick using each leg. Then switch your stance so your right leg is forward, and kick using each leg. Although it sounds complicated, the more you practice, the better you become.

FRONT KICK

The front kick strikes a target directly in front of you. Your foot travels in a straight line from chamber to target, using the ball of your foot to strike. To position your foot in the appropriate way, point your foot and pull your toes back.

To chamber the kick, lift your leg as high as possible, pulling your thigh toward your chest and bending your knee as sharply as possible. Keep your leg slightly in front of your body. This is the chamber position.

Push your leg forward, striking to the target with the ball of your foot. Straighten your leg so that it is completely extended, but do not lock your knee. Thrust your hips forward to help push your foot through the target.

You can vary this kick using different motions. You can snap your front kick, using a whipping motion. Think of snapping your leg out and pulling it back as quickly as possible. Although not as powerful, this kick has the advantage of speed. A variation called the thrust kick allows you to use the entire sole of your foot to kick. You push the target (the opponent) away. Another type of front kick, the instep front kick, uses the instep as the striking surface. In this case, the foot is pointed but the toes are not pulled back. You sweep the kick up toward the target instead of pushing toward the target. The instep front kick is almost always used to kick to the groin (see figures 47 and 48).

Figure 47

Figure 48

SIDE KICK

The side kick uses the bottom of your heel and the outer edge of your foot (sometimes called the "knife edge") to strike. Although your target is in front of you, you turn to face the side in order to perform the technique.

The kick can be used in any stance, but to learn it, start in a front stance. Lift your back leg, bending sharply at the knee. Pivot 90 degrees on your non-kicking foot (called the supporting foot), until your side faces the target. Make sure you pivot on the ball of your foot. Draw your kicking leg forward so that it is slightly in front of your body, keeping the knee bent as much as possible. Tighten your kicking foot so that the sole of your foot is parallel to the floor. This is the chamber position.

Push your kicking leg straight out, extending your leg and straightening but not locking your knee. As you kick, pivot another 90 degrees on your supporting foot, until the heel of your supporting foot faces the target. This foot will have pivoted a total of 180 degrees since you assumed a front stance position. Again, as you pivot balance on the ball of your foot. If you need to, lean slightly over your supporting foot in order to keep your balance.

Strike the target with the heel and outer edge of your foot. Your kicking foot should be turned so that its edge is parallel to the floor. If possible, position your foot so that your toes point slightly down. This concentrates the power of the impact in the heel of your foot, instead of spreading it out over the whole surface area of the bottom of your foot. Never strike the target with your toes pointing upward. Not only is this poor technique, but it can injure your foot (see figures 49 and 50).

Figure 49

Figure 50

JUMP SIDE KICK

The jump side kick adds a jump to the side kick. A step or slide can be used instead of the jump. This kick allows you to quickly cover ground.

Start in a horse stance. The kick is always performed to a target to your side. Your kicking foot is the one closest to the target. Your supporting foot is farthest from the target.

Move your supporting foot toward your kicking leg until it just touches your kicking foot. Chamber your kicking leg by picking it up high and bending the knee 90 degrees. Kick straight out to the side, remembering to keep your foot tight and the edge of your foot parallel to the floor. Strike with the heel and outer edge of your foot, and strike with your toes pointing down, if possible. No pivoting or turning on the supporting foot is necessary.

Once you can execute the technique with a step as described above, replace the step with a jump as you move your supporting leg toward your kicking leg. Jump while chambering your kicking leg. Both legs should be off the ground

Figure 51   **Figure 52**

at the same time. Then strike your target and land with both feet in the horse stance position. You can move from stepping to jumping by executing the step faster and faster as you practice until you get the feel for the movement. Don't worry if it seems to take some time to master this technique. You may be at the intermediate stage before you feel comfortable with it (see figures 51 and 52).

REVERSE SIDE KICK

Most kicks can be done reverse. Instead of kicking directly to your target, you turn in a complete revolution, delivering the strike halfway through the revolution. Then you complete the revolution and return to your starting position. Adding the revolution to the kick slows the kick down, but it also makes the kick much more powerful. Using reverse kicks can also help you win sparring matches, since they add variety to your kicking techniques, making it difficult for your opponent to judge what your next move will be.

The term "reverse kick" in Tae Kwon Do is often used to refer to a reverse side kick, since this is the most common type of reverse kick used, especially at the beginner and intermediate stages of training. The reverse side kick is sometimes called a back side kick.

The reverse side kick can be done from any position, but it is easiest to practice in a horse stance position. In this case, the target is to your side, and your kicking foot is the foot farthest from the target. Shift your weight so that your supporting foot (the one closest to the target) bears most of it. Lift your kicking leg off the ground, bending the knee at least 90 degrees. Tighten your foot; keep the bottom of your foot parallel to the floor. Then, rotate on your supporting foot so that your back faces the target. Turn your head so that you can see the target. Strike as soon as your kicking foot is directly in front of the

Figure 53

Figure 54

Figure 55

target. Strike just as you would with a side kick, using the bottom of your heel and the outer knife edge of your foot as the striking surface. If you have trouble maintaining your balance, lean over your supporting foot. Drive your foot through the target, re-chamber your leg, and continue pivoting on your supporting foot until you return to the starting position. You will have done a complete 360-degree revolution this way. You must move quickly to successfully execute this kick. By swiftly picking up your leg, chambering and pivoting, you gain the momentum to strike and continue through with a complete revolution.

Once you have mastered the reverse kick in the horse stance position, try it in the front or back stance position. In these stances, the target is in front of you, instead of to the side, but the rest of the movement is the same. You chamber your back leg (the one farthest from the target), shift your weight to your forward foot, spin to the back, and deliver the strike, then continue the revolution until you return to your starting position (see figures 53, 54 and 55).

ROUNDHOUSE KICK

The roundhouse kick attacks a target in front of you. The kick comes from the side, moving in an arc. You use the instep of your foot to strike. Although the kick can be performed from any stance, start with a front stance. Lift your back leg up, cock your knee at a 90-degree angle and sweep your leg in an arc moving from the back to the front. Keep the side of your leg horizontal to the ground. As you move, your supporting foot should pivot so that by the time your kicking foot strikes the target, your supporting foot has pivoted 180 degrees. The heel of your supporting foot should face the target. Pivot on the ball of your foot in order to move quickly.

When your knee is in line with the target, snap your foot out, straightening your leg.

Strike the target with the top of your foot. Keep your toes pointed and tighten your foot at the moment of impact (see figures 56 and 57).

Several variations of this technique can be used in different circumstances. When striking a hard, solid surface, such as for board-breaking exhibitions, use the breaking technique: pull your toes back and strike the target with the ball of your foot. You execute the kick itself in exactly the same way.

A short roundhouse kick moves directly to the target in a straight line, without traveling in an arc. The instep of the foot is still used as the striking surface. This is faster than the traditional roundhouse kick, although not as powerful. The thrust roundhouse kick adds power by thrusting the hips into the kick as the kick lands. The supporting foot pivots slightly beyond 180 degrees for this kick.

Figure 56

Figure 57

CRESCENT KICKS

Like crescent blocks, crescent kicks use a circular movement, either going from the inside to the outside motion or from the outside to the inside. If you're moving from the outside to the inside, you use the inner edge of your foot to strike. If you're moving from the inside to the outside, you use the outer edge of your foot. A variation — the axe kick — uses the heel of the foot and can be performed using an inside-to-outside movement or an outside-to-inside movement.

In a crescent kick, the kicking leg travels in a semi-circle, moving up, across the body, and down. The kicking leg remains completely extended. The knee never bends. Crescent kicks are always used to strike a high target area, such as shoulder, neck and head.

Inside-to-Outside Crescent Kick

Start in a front stance. Lift your back leg up and sweep it inward. Bring your leg across your body as you swing it up as high as you can. Once you've reached the highest point you can kick, strike to the target, which should be in front of you, using the outer edge of your foot. Finish the kick by smoothly bringing your leg back down to the starting position.

For this kick to be most effective, bring your foot up just slighly to the side of the target, then swing your foot through the target (see figures 59 and 60).

Figure 58   Figure 59

Figure 60   Figure 61

Outside-to-Inside Crescent Kick

Start in a front stance. Lift your leg behind you, sweep it to the side and then forward. As you perform this motion, bring your leg up as high as possible. Your foot should reach its highest point when it is almost directly in front of you. Strike the target with the inner edge of your foot. Finish the movement by bringing your leg back smoothly to the beginning position (see figures 60 and 61).

Axe Kick

The axe kick is more powerful than a simple crescent kick. It uses the back of your heel to strike instead of the edge of the foot. To perform an axe kick, begin with a crescent kick (either inside-to-outside or outside-to-inside). As your kick reaches its highest point in the arc, pull your leg *down* sharply instead of continuing the circular movement to the side. Use your heel to strike the top of the target. Then continue through and return your foot to its starting position (see figure 62).

Figure 62

PART THREE:
PRACTICING TAE KWON DO:
INTERMEDIATE

10

INTERMEDIATE STANCES

Most of the stances in Tae Kwon Do you learned as a beginner. At the intermediate stage, only the T-stance is a new addition. However, at this stage, you learn to turn while in various stances, and you learn the fundamentals of body shifting and footwork.

T-STANCE

The T-stance is an exaggerated form of the back stance. It can be used to add an additional thrust to hand techniques. To turn a back stance into a T-stance, simply slide your front foot forward. Your position should resemble that of a horse stance, except that your feet remain perpendicular to each other. Bend both knees to a 90 degree angle, and reposition your body weight so that each foot bears

Figure 63

an equal amount. You can slide into the T-stance whenever you're in a back stance or a fighting stance; this can increase your punching range. By sliding in, you can strike to the chest, then retreat to the back stance to defend against any countering move your opponent might make (see figure 63).

BODY SHIFTING

In addition to actually blocking an opponent's attacks, you can defend yourself in other ways. Body shifting, one of the easiest defensive techniques to learn, means you merely move your body out of the way to avoid an attack. You can do this without expending a lot of effort blocking. Practice body shifting by turning your chest away from oncoming strikes. Have a partner punch or kick to your chest. Pivot at the waist to avoid the strikes. To add another level of difficulty, ask your partner to occasionally punch at your head instead of your body. In this case, simply turn or pull your head back to avoid the punch. When you practice body shifting, try not to move your feet. Remain in your stance position, but let the attack slip by, leaving you in an excellent position to respond (see figure 64).

Figure 64

STANCE TURNING

Sometimes it is not enough to simply move your body out of the way of an attack. Occasionally, your opponent might circle around behind you, and you'll need to shift position to see what your opponent intends to do. In this case, the more smoothly and more quickly you can turn, while still maintaining your stance, the easier you can defend against your opponent and prepare to counterattack.

When your opponent circles looking for an opening to strike, don't respond by also circling. This wastes energy and gives control of the fight to your opponent. In some competitions, circling is grounds for disqualification. Instead of circling, simply shift the direction you face. Pick up your back leg, and pivot on your front foot. If you need to make a complete 180-degree shift, simply pivot both feet while turning your chest and your hips in the new direction. Your back leg will become your front leg and your front leg will become your back leg. Depending on the stance you're in, you may need to redistribute your weight. Stance turning often seems complicated at first, but it is quite simple; it just requires practice. By doing this, you'll save your energy for   attacking and blocking. You will also be able to concentrate on defeating your opponent if you don't get drawn into circling, too (see figures 65, 66, 67 and 68).

FOOTWORK

Footwork refers to the position and movement of your feet. By following certain footwork patterns, you can move into and out of fighting range against an opponent. Footwork also helps you avoid your opponent's techniques. Prac-

Figure 65

Figure 66

Figure 67

Figure 68

tice each pattern repeatedly, both separately and as a part of your sparring practice. This will help you understand the purpose of each pattern. If you have a partner, she can punch or kick at you while you practice footwork techniques.

Forward Stepping

Use forward stepping (also called straight stepping) when you need to move into kicking or punching range. Slide your front foot forward, then slide your back foot forward. Practice making small, quick sliding movements toward your target. Be prepared to stop your forward motion in a split-second, in case your opponent responds to your movement. To cover your movement, you can perform a front kick with your forward leg, then set your foot down closer to your opponent (rather than re-cham-

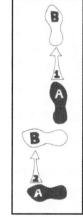

Figure 69

bering it and returning it to the starting position). Then slide your back foot forward (see figure 69).

Variation:

Forward step by bringing your back foot forward and making it your front foot. Slide your new back foot into proper fighting stance position (see figure 70).

Backward Stepping

Use backward stepping to get out of range of your opponent's attacks and to move into punching or kicking range if you're too close to your opponent to attack effectively. Slide your back foot backward, then your front foot. Practice this technique using quick sliding movements. Again, you can use a front kick to cover your movement. In this case, use your front leg to kick, then set your kicking foot down next to your back foot and slide your back foot back (see figure 71).

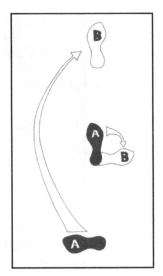

Figure 70

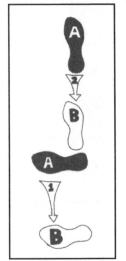

Figure 71

Variation:

Backward step by bringing your front foot back and making it your back foot. Slide your new front foot into proper fighting stance position (see figure 72).

Combining Forward and Backward Stepping

Combine forward stepping and backward stepping to move into and out of fighting range. Be sure you *don't* get into a rhythm (i.e., two forward steps, two backward steps, two forward steps) because this is easy for an opponent to respond to. Instead, vary the way you combine the two techniques so that your opponent cannot predict whether you're coming or going.

Side Stepping

Use this pattern to move out of the way of a direct attack. Instead of stepping backward, use a quick step to the side. Unlike backward stepping, side stepping keeps you in range so that you can immediately counter your

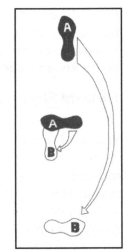

Figure 72

opponent's attack. To step left, simply slide your forward foot to the left and follow with your back foot. Again, use a sliding motion that can easily be stopped and re-directed in case you need to respond to a movement on your opponent's part (see figure 73).

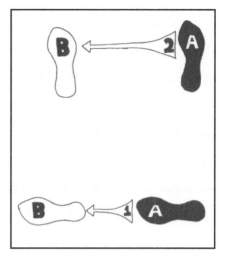

Figure 73

You must move in the direction *opposite* the strike in order to evade it. There-fore, if a kick is coming toward the left side of your body, you must move to the right. Otherwise, you will step into the kick and suffer for it. Practice sidestepping a vari-ety of techniques so that you can get a sense of the intended target area of a strike be-fore you try to avoid it. Once you can avoid a strike by sidestepping it, add a countering technique of your own. For ex-ample, if your opponent punches toward your right shoulder and you step to the left, you can deliver a side kick to her now-exposed ribs. Practice the sidestepping and the countering moves repeatedly, until you feel comfortable with them. Then incorporate them into your sparring practice.

11

INTERMEDIATE BLOCKS

The intermediate Tae Kwon Do practitioner learns only a few blocks. However, she adds to her knowledge of defensive techniques by building her understanding of how blocking can set up an effective counterattack.

Use intermediate blocks, more sophisticated than the basic, beginner blocks, in more complex situations. You must begin to distinguish between various types of attack and learn to react appropriately to different strikes targeted at different areas of the body.

SINGLE FOREARM BLOCK

The forearm block protects the middle section. It can be performed in any stance, but it is easiest to learn in a back stance. Your forward arm does the blocking. Extend your back arm slightly in front of your body in order to "pull" and force your forward arm farther forward. Begin with your forward arm resting on its opposite shoulder. Your hand should be in a fist with the palm facing up toward the ceiling. Sweep your blocking arm across your body, keeping your elbow bent 90 degrees. Keep your upper arm almost parallel to the floor throughout the entire technique. Pull

Figure 74

your non-blocking arm back to your waist. As you block, twist the wrist of your blocking hand so that your palm faces away from your body. The fleshy part of your forearm is the blocking surface (see figures 74 and 75).

DOUBLE FOREARM BLOCK, MIDDLE SECTION

This block is a variation of the forearm block. One arm blocks the attack while the other arm protects your chest and midsection.

Practice this technique in a front stance. Make both hands into fists. Reach behind you with both arms. Your forward arm should reach back across your body, palm facing down. Your back arm should extend straight behind you, also with palm facing down. Sweep both arms forward at the same time.

Figure 75

Stop your forward arm just as it passes over the top of your front leg; your elbow should be at a 90-degree angle. Your back arm should cross your chest. Rest your back fist in your front forearm, near the elbow. This augments the block, making it more powerful, and also protects your midsection from attack. Twist both wrists just at the end of the block so that both palms face the ceiling (see figure 76 and 77).

DOUBLE FOREARM BLOCK, LOW SECTION

The double forearm block can be used to block the low section as well, using a slightly different technique. It is easiest to practice this technique in a

Figure 76

Figure 77

Figure 78   **Figure 79**

back stance, although it can be used in any stance. To block to the low section, reach behind and up instead of reaching directly behind you with your hands. The technique is performed similarly to the double knife hand block, low section.

Both hands should be fists. The palm of your forward hand should face the ceiling, while the palm of your back hand should face down. Your forward elbow will be bent, but your back arm should be straight.

Sweep both arms down simultaneously. Straighten your forward arm while twisting at the wrist so that your palm faces in. Stop the block just beyond your forward knee. The forward blocking arm should be 6 to 8 inches in front of your knee and slightly to the side.

As you bring your back arm down, twist your wrist so that your palm faces up. Rest your back fist near your midsection, slightly in front of your chest. This blocks an attack to the lower section, such as your knee or groin, while still protecting your midsection (see figures 78 and 79).

C-BLOCK

The block protects your middle section and your head at the same time. Your arms resemble the letter "C" at the end position. Visualize it as a high block and a forearm block done simultaneously. Although it can be performed in any stance, it is easiest to learn in a back stance.

Make both hands into fists. Chamber both fists slightly above your back hip. Rest your front fist just above your back fist. Twist your wrists so that both palms face up to the ceiling.

Block with both hands simultaneously. Sweep your forward arm across your body, stopping at your front leg. Twist your wrist as you block so that your palm and the fleshy part of your forearm face out, just as in a forearm

Figure 80   **Figure 81**

block. Keep your upper arm almost parallel to the ground and keep your elbow cocked at a 90 degree angle. Remember, you should be able to see over your fist.

At the same time, sweep your back arm up to protect your head, as in a high block. Twist your wrist outward so that your palm and the fleshy part of your forearm face away from you. (This is the blocking surface and will absorb the blow.) Keep your arm a few inches above and slightly in front of the top of your head. Your elbow should remain at a 90-degree angle (see figures 80 and

Figure 82   **Figure 83**

81).

OPEN HAND C-BLOCK

A variation of the C-block is the open hand C-block. You perform it in exactly the same way as the basic C-block. The only difference is in the position of your hands. Make both hands into knife hands and perform the block with your hands in this position (see figures 82 and 83).

PRACTICING BLOCKS

When you practice blocks, perform them quickly and sharply. Your blocks should be just as powerful as your kicks and your punches. Pay careful attention to the blocking surface, usually the fleshy part of your forearm. If you use your wrist or the back of your arm, you could break one of your bones. For this reason, remember to add the twist at the end of each block, which puts your arm in the correct position.

To sharpen your blocking skills, ask a partner to attack different target areas of your body. Respond with an appropriate block. If your block is unsuccessful, or you choose the wrong block, stop and discuss how this could be improved. If you don't have a martial arts partner, anyone can simply call out "head" or "knee" at random, and you can perform an appropriate block to defend that area.

BUILDING ON BLOCKS

When you practice blocks, build on your skills by using blocks not just as simple defensive manuevers but also as methods for setting up an attack sequence of your own. As you practice your blocks, think of ways you can launch an attack immediately after the block. Consider, for example, a low block. When you push an opponent's kick or punch out of the way, it often exposes a target area. Take the opportunity to strike to the unguarded area. Or when you block with a high block, push your opponent off balance, perhaps even sliding a foot behind her ankle to trip her. (This technique is not legal in sparring, but could be useful in a confrontation.) Therefore, when you perform a block, consider the attacking techniques you can perform with your non-blocking hand or with your feet, and add them to your practice routine.

Also, consider how others might use blocks against you. If you know that someone blocking your kick might follow with a strike, you should keep your guard up. When you're sparring, an opponent may try to force you to perform a block so that you'll leave a target area open. After setting you up in this way, the opponent will attack with the technique she intended to all along. Because of this, make sure you perform your blocks with the forward arm, leaving your back arm guarding your body (and in position to guard your head, if necessary.) Also, let the opponent's technique come to you. Some beginning and intermediate fighters "chase" the technique in order to block it, leaning forward or striking out to move the technique away. This causes you to lose balance and leaves you vulnerable to attack. Block only when the strike will land if you don't. In addition, practice techniques such as body shifting, stance turning, and footwork that don't require you to commit to a major blocking movement that can give the advantage to your opponent.

12

INTERMEDIATE HAND STRIKING TECHNIQUES

At the intermediate stage of Tae Kwon Do, defensive techniques become less important and attacking techniques are emphasized. Although Tae Kwon Do is perceived as a kicking art, it incorporates many hand techniques, most of which are introduced at the intermediate level. This does not mean you should give up working on defensive techniques. Rather, it means you have more work to do, learning to balance offensive and defensive techniques, strategies and tactics.

At the intermediate stage, you should begin more serious sparring with partners, making this a more significant part of your workout.

KNIFE HAND STRIKE

This technique uses the outer edge of your hand (the little finger edge) as the striking surface, with your hand in a knife hand position, fingers tight and straight.

Make your hand into a knife hand by tightening and straightening your fingers. Check that there are no gaps between your fingers. Keep your thumb firmly against your hand, bending the knuckle at 90-degree angle. Chamber your knife hand, palm up, above the opposite side shoulder, near your ear. Your non-striking hand should be in a fist, extended slightly in front of your body.

Sweep your striking arm across your body, straightening your elbow as you go. At the target, twist your wrist so your palm faces down to create a more powerful impact. Pull your non-striking hand back to your side to add additional power to your strike (see figures 84 and 85 on the following page).

Figure 84

Figure 85

Figure 86

Figure 87

45-Degree Knife Hand Strike

To create a quicker strike, use this simple variation of the knife hand strike. Chamber your knife hand, palm up, near the *same* side shoulder. Position your hand so that your elbow is at a 45-degree angle. Strike forward and down, extending your elbow. Your elbow should remain in a 45-degree angle as you strike your target. Because there is no wrist twist to this technique, it is not as powerful or as explosive as the traditional knife hand strike, but you can deliver it more quickly (see figures 86 and 87).

RIDGE HAND STRIKE

The ridge hand strike, although similar to the knife hand strike, differs in two ways: you hold your hand in a slightly different position, and you strike with the inner edge (thumb edge) of your hand. To make a ridge hand, tighten and straighten your fingers so they are fully extended with no gaps between them. Fold your thumb *under* your hand so that the edge of your hand is smooth.

You will strike with this edge.

To perform a ridge hand, simply extend your ridge hand straight out to the side, horizontal to the ground. Make sure your arm is fully extended, but don't lock your elbow as you can injure it on impact. Sweep your arm across your body, pivoting at the waist and hips as you do so. Strike the target with the inner edge of your hand (see figures 88 and 89).

Reverse Ridge Hand Strike

This variation of the ridge hand strike begins with the ridge hand positioned under the opposite arm, palm down. Extend your non-striking arm in front of your body. Sweep your striking arm out toward your target, moving away from your body. Keep your elbow slightly bent throughout the entire strike. At the last moment, twist your wrist so that your palm faces up, striking with the thumb edge of your hand (see figures 91 and 92).

Figure 88   **Figure 89**

Figure 90   **Figure 91**

BACK FIST STRIKE

This technique uses the back of the fist as the striking surface to attack a high target area. Start by making a fist with your hand. Chamber your fist above the opposite shoulder, near your ear. Position your fist with the palm facing outward. Sweep your arm outward, away from your body. Twist your wrist at the moment of impact so that the back of your fist strikes the target area (see figures 92 and 93).

Figure 92

Figure 93

HAMMER FIST STRIKE

The hammer fist, also called bottom fist, is a deceptively simple technique. The bottom of the hand, the striking surface, is used like a hammer. To perform the technique, chamber your fist above the same side shoulder, with the bottom of your hand facing up and out. Sweep your hand down so that the bottom of your fist strikes the target. This downward strike is only used when striking from above a target area; variations below offer alternatives depending on the target area (see figures 94 and 95 on the following page).

Horizontal Hammer Fist Strike

The horizontal hammer fist strike aims at a target beside you. Begin with your fist chambered above the opposite shoulder. Keeping your fist in the hammer fist position, palm up, sweep outward across your body. Your arm should remain parallel to the floor. At the moment of impact, twist your wrist so that your palm faces down. This adds additional power to the strike (see figures 96 and 97 on the following page).

Backward Hammer Fist Strike

For targets to the back, use a backward hammer fist strike. Chamber your hand, in the hammer fist position, near the same side shoulder. The bottom of

Figure 94

Figure 95

Figure 96

Figure 97

your fist should face outward and upward. Sweep downward, straightening your arm and elbow. This technique works well to strike to the groin. To strike higher, keep your elbow partially bent. To make this a more powerful technique, turn your shoulder and upper body into it, or step back as you strike (see figures 98 and 99 on the following page).

GENERATING POWER

As discussed earlier, women tend to have less upper body strength than men. This means women have to pay more attention to creating power when using hand techniques.

Because many elements work together to make up a good hand strike (hand position, push/pull technique, twisting your wrist), you can spend too much time worrying about perfect execution. This can slow your techniques down,

Figure 98

Figure 99

make you feel hestitant, and rob your strikes of much of their power. To solve this problem, always strike with confidence. The result may not be a perfect hand strike, and you may make a mistake in the execution, but if you have confidence behind your techniques, your techniques will be more powerful and more controlled.

The beginner section described techniques for improving upper body power. Once you have incorporated these beginning methods into your training, add the techniques that follow to increase your power.

Using Your Body Weight

Many beginning martial artists perform hand techniques using only their hand and their arm. This does not create very powerful strikes. At the interme-

Figure 100

diate level, you should begin to use your body weight to create more power behind your punches. Often, martial artists try to create more power by "reaching" with their arms, rolling their shoulders forward. Not only is this ineffective, it causes you to lose balance and makes you an easier target for an opponent (see figure 100).

Instead of reaching with your arm in order to get more power, twist at the hips as you chamber your strike, then uncoil as you execute the strike. This spring-like action puts the weight of your chest and hips into the strike, making it more powerful. For example, suppose you're practicing a punch, and you're using your right hand as the punching hand.

Chamber your hand at your waist, but turn your chest to the right as well, so that your left side and your left shoulder are slightly forward. Then, pull back with your left hand as you uncoil and strike with your right hand. Always keep your shoulder and chest in the same plane. That is, don't pull your arm way back in order to generate power, while leaving your chest facing forward. Instead, think of your arm, shoulder and chest in a line. While you can pull the whole line back and move it forward, you shouldn't pull parts of the line back or move parts of it forward.

Stepping into the Strike

Stepping into a strike also generates power. A step puts the weight of your entire body behind a single technique, giving you explosive power. To practice this, assume a front stance position. Prepare to strike with a straight punch, using the same side hand as your forward leg. (If your left leg is forward, punch with your left hand.) Chamber your hand at your waist. Remember to twist your wrist so your palm faces up. Have your opposite arm slightly extended in front of your body in order to perform the push/pull technique. Twist your upper body back to add impact to your strike. Finally, slide your forward foot back about 8 inches. Unleash your strike, uncoiling at the waist, stepping forward, and striking in one continuous movement. You may find this difficult to do at first. By practicing the elements separately, then together (going as slowly as you need), you will soon gain proficiency.

Adding these power-generating movements to your strikes will maximize the amount of power you can generate with a single strike.

13

ELBOW AND KNEE
STRIKING TECHNIQUES

Tae Kwon Do practitioners rely primarily on their hands and their feet to strike, but at the intermediate level they learn to use additional body parts: the knees and the elbows. While these techniques cannot be used in official sparring matches, they make useful additions to your martial arts arsenal. Elbow and knee strikes serve as excellent weapons in self-defense situations, especially when your attacker is in close range.

ELBOW STRIKES

Elbow strikes use either the point of the elbow or the forearm just in front of the elbow joint as the striking surface. You can perform elbow strikes in any stance, but to learn the techniques, begin in a front stance.

Forward Elbow Strike

This technique is used for targets directly in front of you. Extend your arm out to the side, then bend your elbow in as tightly as possible. Your bent arm should remain about shoulder high, parallel to the floor. The striking surface is the front of your elbow.

Pivot at your waist, reaching behind you as far as possible with your bent arm. Uncoil at the waist, sweeping foward with your arm. Strike through the target by continuing to pivot through.

To strike different target areas, don't move your arm, move your legs. Assume a lower stance with your knees bent more for a lower target; a higher stance with your knees bent less for a higher target. Targets that are very low or very high require a different kind of elbow strike (see figures 101 and 102).

TAE KWON DO FOR WOMEN

Figure 101

Figure 102

Backward Elbow Strike

This technique is used to strike targets behind you, using the point of your elbow. To perform it, make a fist and bring your striking arm forward. Cover your fist with your non-striking hand; this arm will help push your elbow through the target.

Look to see your target, then drive your elbow backward. The point of your elbow should strike the target and create the impact. You can increase the power of this technique by bringing the striking arm farther forward and by stepping backward as you strike ("stepping into the strike"). See figures 103 and 104.

Figure 103

Figure 104

88

Variation:

You can strike to a target to your side, instead of behind you, using the same technique. Simply point your elbow toward the target, bring your arm slightly forward to generate more power, then drive it into the target.

Upward Elbow Strike

Use the upward elbow strike for high targets, especially the underside of an opponent's chin. Bend your arm tightly, and reach back. Then sweep your elbow upward. Strike the target from below with the front of your elbow. Guide your arm so that your fist ends up beside your head, near your ear (see figures 105 and 106).

Figure 105   **Figure 106**

Downward Elbow Strike

Although beloved of professional wrestlers, this is actually a legitimate martial arts technique. Raise your arm so that your upper arm is almost parallel to the floor. Bend your elbow at a 90-degree angle. Make your hand a fist. Reach up slightly with your arm, positioning your arm so that the point of your elbow is directly above the target area, then drive your elbow downward through the target. To add power or to strike a very low target, bend both knees as you strike (see figure 107).

Figure 107

KNEE STRIKES

Knee strikes are the simplest, most effective self-defense weapons you'll ever use. Just hit the target with your knee. Because of the power of your lower body and the comparative weakness of the targets you generally aim at (ribs, nose, groin), it doesn't matter if your technique is perfect for it to be effective.

When you peform knee strikes, you can increase the power of your strike by pulling the target toward you as you drive your knee into the target. For example, grab an opponent's head behind the ears and pull

Figure 108

down as you drive your knee into his nose, or grab your opponent's clothing and pull toward you (see figure 108).

Knee strikes can be performed in any stance, but a front stance or fighting stance is usually the most effective position. Knee strikes are most effective in close; kicks and punches are more effective at longer ranges.

Straight Knee Strike

Use the front of your knee cap as the striking surface. Bend your back leg so that your knee is at a 90-degree angle. Swing your leg forward, driving your knee directly into the target (see figure 109).

Roundhouse Knee Strike

This knee strike is similar to the roundhouse kick, except that you're much closer to your opponent. Lift your back leg off the floor. Bend your knee at a 90-degree angle. As you strike, keep the side of your leg parallel to the floor.

Figure 109

Figure 110

Sweep your leg from the side toward the target, pivoting slightly on your supporting foot as you do so. Drive your knee into the target (see figure 110).

CREATING POWERFUL ELBOW AND KNEE STRIKES

These attacking techniques usually aren't allowed in sparring matches, because they can be dangerous. Nonetheless, they can be used very effectively in self-defense and should be practiced as part of your normal martial arts routine.

To improve the effectiveness of these strikes, think speed rather than power. When martial artists have difficulty generating power with these techniques, they usually think they're not strong enough or that they need to "push" harder, using brute strength for the techniques to be effective. This is not the case. Elbow and knee strikes rely on speed. For female martial artists, this is good news; we tend to be faster than our male counterparts, and speed generates power just as mass does.

In practice, strike the target as quickly as possible without cheating the follow through, and return to the starting position, prepared to strike again. Try to return to the starting position faster than you strike. This creates the speed you must have for effective knee and elbow strikes. As a drill, time how long it takes for you to perform 10 elbow strikes with sufficient power to stop or injure an attacker and work to beat that time.

14

INTERMEDIATE KICKING TECHNIQUES

At the intermediate level, you build on the basic kicking techniques you've learned. For example, you will learn a jump front kick that adds a more advanced element to the basic front kick. If you haven't learned the front kick very well, the jump front kick will be much more difficult for you to master.

You learn more kicks at the intermediate level than at any other, so you must be patient and practice each new technique equally. Try not to feel overwhelmed by the amount you have to learn. Some of the techniques will seem more difficult than others, but with practice you can become comfortable performing all of these kicks.

Intermediate Tae Kwon Do artists must work on their basic kicking techniques until the kicks are second nature and can be performed without thought. Improve your kicking techniques by practicing, paying careful attention to appropriate execution — and practicing some more.

As with any technique, you must kick with confidence. Even if your kick is not perfect, striking with confidence adds power to your techniques.

Incorporate slow practice into your training. Watch yourself perform your techniques (a mirror is essential for this; a video camera helpful). Practice each kick at least 10 times on each leg during every workout session. Do not forget to chamber your kick before beginning the strike, to strike accurately and with the correct striking surface, to follow through on the strike, and to return your leg to its chamber position instead of just letting your foot fall to the ground.

The chamber or starting position of your leg is the most important element of an effective technique. If your starting position is incorrect, there is no way your kick can be performed adequately. Each kick has a different chamber position, but you should always raise your leg as far as you can and bend your knee tightly if appropriate. Even if your target is low, start your leg in a high, tight chamber position to generate power. A good chamber helps you kick to high target areas even if your flexibility needs work.

The next most important element of a good kick is the re-chamber — returning your kick to the starting position. Re-chambering your leg leaves you in position to strike again or to return to your beginning stance. The effort of re-chambering your kicks adds snap and speed to the kicking technique itself. In addition, the kick looks better — sharp and confident instead of sloppy. The re-chamber builds your muscle strength.

Take a extra few seconds to re-chamber your leg and return to your starting stance instead of simply dropping your foot to the floor after you've done your kick.

ADDING SPEED TO KICKS

Women's lower bodies tend to be stronger than our upper bodies, and our natural flexibility helps us reach up higher with our kicks. Speed is another of our advantages. Kicking quickly makes your kicks more powerful and less likely to be spotted and blocked. Kicking swiftly keeps you agile, ready for your next move. If you kick slowly, your opponent can see your kicks coming and can prepare to block or counterattack.

Since women tend to be naturally faster than men, it makes sense to build on your speed. Add speed to your kicks by adding a whipping or snapping motion to the end of the kick. Instead of pushing or sweeping with your kick, snap it at the moment of impact. Cracking a whip adds impact; so does snapping a kick.

Speed up your kicks by returning your kick to the starting position as fast as or faster than you performed the kick. Work on kicking forward and then pulling your leg back instead of relying on momentum to do the work for you.

Try counting out loud for each kick. To increase your speed, count faster and keep pace with your count. Use a tape recorder for an extra challenge. That way, you can't cheat when you're counting. A helper, even a non-martial artist, can call out a count and urge you to keep up with the pace she sets.

ADDING HEIGHT TO KICKS

Improve your reach and add height to your kicks by increasing your flexibility and leg strength. You need both: one without the other won't help. Leg strength is necessary to perform a kick head high without dropping your foot or your leg. Without flexibility, you won't be able to reach the high target area, no matter how strong you are.

There are some simple, straightforward ways to address the strength and flexibility issue. You can perform stretches to improve your flexibility and perform weight training exercises to increase your strength. These take time to work, but you can immediately improve your performance by concentrating on executing chambers correctly and by practicing high kicks. In order to challenge yourself, have a helper hold a target for you to repeatedly kick toward, raising the target a few inches after each successful kick.

Martial artists know a few ways you can add height to your kicks. Adding these techniques to your kicks can immediately improve your skills.

1.) Balance on the ball of your supporting foot. Some martial artists incorrectly balance on the heel of their supporting foot, which actually subtracts height from their kicks. Others stay flat-footed, using the sole of their supporting foot. This keeps them firmly on the ground. Instead, learn to balance on the ball of your supporting foot. You'll be able to reach higher and farther with your kicks.

2.) Pivot completely when you perform a kick that requires it. For example, a side kick requires you to pivot 180 degrees on your supporting foot. Many martial artists pivot 45 or 90 degrees; some barely pivot at all. Not only is this poor technique, it's hard on your knees and your hips. Instead, concentrate on pivoting smoothly through the entire strike.

3.) Lift the heel of your supporting foot off the ground as you strike. This adds additional inches to your height. For stationery kicks such as the front kick, you can go so far as to stand on your toes.

4.) For kicks that require a pivot, add additional height by leaning over your supporting foot.

These quick fixes can add several inches to the height of your kicks, meaning that you can strike to higher targets even if you're a shorter-than-average woman. The four fixes described above are actually correct and appropriate martial arts techniques and should be used even after you've gained additional strength and flexibility.

DOUBLE KICKS

To add another dimension to your sparring techniques, use double kicks. Perform two kicks in a row without setting your foot down between kicks. Often, your opponent will block or evade your first kick, but will not expect the second kick. By not setting your leg down, you can increase the speed of your second kick.

You can use double kicks to strike to different target areas. Your first kick might be to the midsection, drawing your opponent's hands and guard down; your second kick would then strike directly to your opponent's unguarded head.

Although practitioners often use the same kick when performing double kicks (for instance, two roundhouses in a row), you can also vary the kicks. Try a roundhouse kick followed by a sidekick or a front kick followed by a round-house kick.

Any direct kick, such as a front kick, side kick and roundhouse kick can be performed double. Circular kicks, such as crescent kicks, cannot.

HOOKING KICK

The hooking kick uses the back of the heel as the striking surface. It is usually aimed high, at the shoulder or the head. Although it can be performed in any stance, learn it in the horse stance position. In this case, your target is to the side. In any other stance, your target will be to the front.

The leg closest to the target is the kicking leg. Chamber your kicking leg as you would for a side kick, lifting your knee high, bending it sharply, and tightening your foot so that the sole is parallel to the floor. Extend your leg and straighten your knee so that your foot goes slightly in front of and past the target area. Then snap your foot back to the target, so that the back of your heel strikes the target.

In a back stance or front stance position, you would simply pivot on your supporting foot and perform the kick like a sidekick, except that you add a hooking motion to the end of the kick. This hooking motion is the actual strike

Figure 111

Figure 112

Figure 113

(see figures 111, 112 and 113).

SPINNING WHEEL KICK

This technique, also called the spinning heel kick, fascinates non-martial artists who think it must be extremely difficult to do. It is not that hard to do, nor does it require special physical ability. All you need is practice.

Start in a back stance with your forward shoulder facing the target. Your back leg, the one the farthest from the target, is the kicking leg. The back of your heel is the striking surface.

Pivot, spinning backward, on your supporting foot. Extend your back leg straight out, keeping your knee straight throughout the entire technique. Keep your heel straight by bending your ankle at a 90-degree angle. Lean over your supporting foot as you spin, both to keep your balance and to reach higher with your kicking leg. Spin through the target, striking with the back of your heel, and return to the starting position (see figures 114, 115, 116 and 117).

Your heel should strike head- or shoulder-high. If you're incapable of this at first, don't panic. It will come with practice.

You must generate a lot of speed as you spin in order to complete the revolution while kicking high and hard. To add speed, at the start of the kick, twist your waist so that your back shoulder comes forward. Then uncoil quickly, shifting your weight to your supporting foot and whipping your kicking foot around. Remember to always keep your leg straight. Don't bend your knee or you'll hook your leg, making the strike less effective. Keep your heel tight by bending your ankle. Strike the target with the back of your heel. If you roll your foot, you'll strike the target with your ankle, which can be painful, not to mention dangerous.

JUMPING KICKS

Many of the kicking techniques you learn at the intermediate level require a jump. The purpose is twofold: to add height and to add power. Without jumping you can only kick as high as you can reach, and the more you have

Figure 114

Figure 115

Figure 116

Figure 117

to reach with your leg, the less power you have. By adding a jump, you can get additional height without losing power. In addition, whenever you incorporate a jump into a kicking technique, you increase the amount of damage you can do. This is good news for women in that it levels the playing field. If you can perform a jumping kick against an attacker, you can stop even a much larger person.

The drawback, of course, is that women have a lower center of gravity than men and much of our weight is concentrated in our hips and abdominal area, which interferes with our ability to jump. However, these drawbacks can be overcome through practice and with a thorough understanding of each technique. Remember, you don't have to jump head-high (or even waist-high) in order to perform a jumping technique, although you should always try to improve and master these techniques. Many women find that after weeks, even months, of practice, they suddenly "get" jumping kicks and no longer feel like they have to battle their bodies. Has something changed about their bodies? Probably not. Most likely, something has changed about their minds, and they have decided they can do more difficult techniques even if the techniques were designed with men in mind.

Jump Front Kick

To add a jump to a front kick, stand with your feet together directly in front of your target. Crouch so that your knees bend to a 45-degree angle. Keep your back and shoulders upright. Spring from the crouch, jumping into the air. As soon as you launch into your jump, chamber your kicking leg and strike with the ball of your foot. Practice your timing so that you kick as you reach the highest point of your jump. Intermediate martial artists often kick as they're coming down from the jump, and thereby lose some of their power, height and momentum.

The jump front kick works well to strike the underside of a target, such as under an opponent's chin (see figures 118 and 119).

Figure 118

Figure 119

Jump Reverse Kick

Add a jump to the reverse side kick with this technique. Begin in a back stance, with your forward shoulder facing the target. Your leg farthest from the target is your kicking leg. Bend both knees slightly and spring into the air. As you launch yourself into the air, chamber your back leg and kick into the target with your heel.

Adding the jump to the reverse side kick can make it difficult to perform the necessary revolution. To overcome this problem, twist at the waist so that your back shoulder comes forward. Then, as you jump, uncoil from the shoulder. Think of your back shoulder pulling your body around backward. Chamber your back leg and strike the target (see figures 120, 121 and 122).

| **Figure 120** | **Figure 121** | **Figure 122** |

Jump Roundhouse Kick

To add a jump to the roundhouse kick, begin by standing in front of the target with your feet together. Crouch so that your knees bend to a 45-degree angle. Keep your back and shoulders straight and upright. Spring from the crouch, pivoting slightly on your supporting foot as you leap in order to position your hips correctly for the kick. Chamber your kicking leg and sweep your kick toward the target, striking with the top of your foot.

As with the jump front kick, strike as you reach the height of your jump, instead of kicking before you reach the high point or after you have begun descending. Experiment with different starting positions of your feet until you find the position that best works for you. Your foot position will help position your hips and kicking leg so that you can perform your jump roundhouse kick smoothly, quickly and powerfully (see figures 123 and 124 on the following page).

Figure 123   **Figure 124**

Jump Hooking Kick

Add a jump to the hooking kick just like you added a jump to the side kick as a beginner. Assume a horse stance position. Take a step with your supporting leg so that it lands next to your kicking leg. Extend your kicking leg and perform the hooking kick. As you grow more comfortable with the technique, you can move more quickly, sliding your supporting foot next to your kicking foot. After some practice, you will be able to move quickly enough that you can strike with the hooking kick while your supporting foot is still in the air, thus adding a jump to your kick (see figures 125 and 126).

Figure 125   **Figure 126**

Flying Side Kick

This variation of the side kick covers a lot of ground. Standing 30 or 40 feet from your target, run toward the target, picking up as much speed as possible. While still several feet from the target, jump into the air. Bend the knee of your non-kicking leg, tucking that leg under you. Extend the knee of your kicking leg so that your leg is straight and your heel is facing the target in the correct side kick position. Strike the target with the foot of your extended leg and land with both feet on the ground.

This so-called "flying" variation can be done with almost any kick. Simply allow yourself room to run, then jump

Figure 127

and perform the kick with the momentum you've gained. Soon you'll be flying through the air.

Although this technique is mostly used in demonstrations, its purpose is to allow you to jump over obstacles on the ground and still strike your opponent (see figure 127).

Mastering Jumping Kicks

Although your first few attempts at jumping kicks may seem laughable, if you stick with it, you will soon succeed. Many martial artists struggle at the intermediate stage since the techniques are more difficult, but the exhilaration you feel when you understand one of these techniques is well worth the effort. By working on your techniques at least three times a week, you will see definite improvement within a few weeks, and you'll be able to do most of the techniques in just a few months.

Still, jumping kicks require patience and persistence. To master jumping kicks, break each kick into its component parts: its jump and its kick. Practice jumping first without worrying about the kick. For instance, if you're practicing the jump front kick, you can stand in front of your target, with your feet together, and crouch and jump over and over until you begin to have a sense of the balance and the mechanics that go into the jump. For the reverse kick, try jumping and tucking your legs under you as tightly as possible, making your calves touch your thighs. Not only does this help you jump higher, it makes the jump look good, and it puts your legs in a better position from which to chamber a kick.

As you become confident of the jump, add the kick back in. Start slowly, going faster and faster as you begin to understand how to do the entire technique. Although each jump kick has a slightly different jump, as you master one jump, the others become easier. As you develop better control over your body, you will be able to perform more difficult techniques with less practice.

PART FOUR:
PRACTICING TAE KWON DO:
ADVANCED

15
ADVANCED STANCES

The emphasis at the advanced stage is to master the stances learned earlier and to learn how to modify them to suit your circumstances. For example, while beginning and intermediate martial artists practice and perform the fighting stance exactly as described, by the time you reach the advanced level, you may want to make appropriate modifications. Perhaps your fighting style is more straight-in and offense-oriented. If so, you may turn your hips and chest toward your sparring opponent. Or perhaps you use a lot of jumping and reverse techniques. In this case, modify your fighting stance so that more weight rests on your forward leg. Perhaps you like to use a balance of front leg, back leg and reverse kicks. Modifying your fighting stance so that it resembles a horse stance with only slightly bent knees may be a solution. In fact, many women find that they must modify the fighting stance to accomodate for basic female anatomy — breasts! It can be hard to punch with the back hand while in a traditional back stance or fighting stance. Many women change their stance so that while their hips face the side, their chests face forward. This makes punches and other hand techniques much easier to perform.

CREATING PERFECT STANCES

As you practice the martial arts, you learn that for practical purposes, you sometimes need to shorten a stance or keep your knees only slightly bent. Modifying stances is acceptable, even desirable, during sparring practice and self-defense practice, but should be avoided during forms and techniques practice. When you're practicing a horse stance, for instance, you don't need to practice *not* bending your knees — that comes naturally!

Creating perfect stances requires concentration. A mirror helps, as does a video camera, so that you can see and critique your performance. As you work on your stances, assess your position from the ground up instead of trying to see and correct everything at once. First, are your feet in the correct position? Do your toes point in the correct direction? Are your feet far enough apart? Next, your knees. Is each knee bent correctly, to the appropriate angle? Your legs: Is each leg in the correct position, bearing the right amount of weight? Your body: Are your hips facing correctly? Your chest? Are your shoulders back? Your hands ready to block or strike? Is your head up, eyes level, ready to meet the opponent? Once you're in the correct position, close your eyes and remember what it feels like. Perhaps there's a little strain in your knee. Perhaps you have to work to hold your stomach in and keep your back straight. Memorize such clues for your body to follow the next time you practice the stance.

Creating perfect stances doesn't mean finding the stance that causes no strain. It's about making minute changes in your body position, then holding the correct position long enough to feel it. A perfect stance will probably always be work. If you practice all your stances and haven't broken into a sweat, you're not doing them right.

Figure 128

X-STANCE

The X-stance is used for blocking low strikes and to protect the groin area. Although different hand strikes can be performed from the X-stance, it is not appropriate for most kicking techniques.

To learn the X-stance, assume a front stance position. From there, slide your back foot forward, so that it comes behind the calf of your forward foot. The toes of your back foot should face the heel of your forward foot. Both heels should be off the ground. Both knees should be bent 45 degrees (see figure 128).

FOOTWORK

Footwork should continue to play an important part of your sparring routine. As you gain confidence with your intermediate footwork, you can supplement your routine with additional, more difficult patterns.

Figure 129   **Figure 130**

Pivot Stepping

Use the pivot step to move toward or away from your opponent. Unlike forward and backward stepping, you do not have to make a complete commitment to the direction you plan to travel. Because of this, pivot stepping gives you more flexibility, but it is more difficult to learn.

To pivot step toward your opponent in order to move into fighting range, push off with your rear foot and and pivot toward your opponent on the ball of your front foot (see figures 129 and 130). Be certain that you do not pivot step *into* an opponent's attack. This requires practice.

To pivot step away from your opponent in order to avoid a strike, push off with your forward foot and pivot in a semi-circle on your back foot. Pivot stepping away from an opponent works best when the opponent is overwhelming you and you need to move out of the way without appearing to be retreating. This gives you a moment to regroup and launch your own attack. You can pivot step several times in a row, both moving forward and moving backward. This gives you greater control over your fighting range.

Use pivot stepping in sparring since turning your back on an opponent to avoid a blow, while sometimes tempting, is illegal in sparring competition and dangerous for you.

Crossover Stepping

To cover ground while at the same time keeping your guard up, use the crossover step. To perform this technique, assume a fighting stance position. Step your back foot over your front foot so that your legs are crossed. Then slide what is now your back foot forward, toward your target (in effect, uncrossing your legs). At the end of the step, you should be in a traditional fighting stance, just as when you started, except you'll be closer to your target.

Figure 131

Figure 132

Figure 133

You can vary this technique by adding a kick such as a front kick or a side kick to it. Bring your back foot over your front foot, crossing your legs. As you step forward with what is now your back foot, turn the step into a kick, striking directly to the target. This technique is most effective in sparring if you perform several crossover steps without the kick first; your opponent will not expect a kick the next time he or she sees you begin a crossover step (see figures 131, 132 and 133).

16

ADVANCED BLOCKS

Advanced blocks differ in nature from beginning and intermediate blocks. Several new blocks are specifically designed to defend against weapons. While some basic and intermediate blocks can be used this way, they are meant to be used against a weaponless opponent. For example, the low block could be used to deflect a baseball bat out of the way if someone were to attack you with baseball bat, but its essential purpose is to block an opponent's kick.

The weapons blocks help you defend against old fashioned weapons — the spear and the staff. It's unlikely that you'll ever have to defend yourself against one of these weapons, but you might have to defend against other weapons, and it's a good idea to consider how you might do this. It's never reasonable to assume that a weaponless fighter will prevail over someone with a gun or a knife, so the most sensible course of action is always to escape a situation before someone brings out a weapon. Nonetheless, as you practice weapons blocks, think about situations in which such a block could be used without resulting in serious injury to you. As the self-defense chapters (Part 6) recommend, practice such scenarios instead of assuming you'll know the right technique to perform when the time comes. Martial arts supply stores sell realistic-looking plastic guns and knives that can be used in weapons training; they give you a slightly better understanding of how to defend against a person with a real weapon. Again, it should be emphasized that a weaponless person cannot expect to prevail over a person with a weapon, regardless of her martial arts training. This is not to say that resigning yourself to violence is the solution. Instead, educate yourself as much as possible, understand your strengths and abilities, and practice, practice, practice.

STAFF BLOCK

The staff block is used to protect against a staff or stick. Perform the block in a back stance position. The staff you're blocking is in line with your front shoulder. Chamber your hands near your back hip, both hands as fists. Your forward hand rests below your back hand. Your forward hand faces palm down, while your back hand faces palm up.

Simultaneously thrust both hands forward. Your back hand should rise near the top of your head, several inches in front your body. As this hand moves, twist your wrist so that your palm faces down and make the fist into the staff block position. Flatten your palm. Keep your fingers tightly together. Spread your thumb as far apart as possible from the rest of your hand to catch the staff in the curve between your thumb and your fingers.

As you block with your back hand, sweep your forward hand across your body so that it stops several inches in front of your forward leg. Twist your wrist so that your palm faces up, and put your hand in the staff block position. Both of your hands should be parallel to each other and about 30 inches apart. The palm of your top hand should face down and the palm of your bottom hand should face up.

The staff block can be varied depending on circumstances. For example, if the stick is smaller, you would close the distance between your hands. With a partner, practice different methods of defending against a stick or staff by building on the basic technique (see figures 134 and 135).

Figure 134   **Figure 135**

X-BLOCK

The X-block defends against a stick coming directly down at you. In a back stance, chamber your hands at your sides in the knife hand position, palms facing up. Thrust both hands up and away from your head, crossing your wrists. Catch the stick between your hands (see figures 136 and 137 on the following page).

Figure 136

Figure 137

SPEAR BLOCK

Although this technique is used to defend against a spear, it can be effective against a knife, and it can be used to block and hold kicks. It is best performed in a front stance.

Assume a front stance position with both hands as fists. Your back hand will do the actual blocking. Extend your forward arm slightly in front of you to counterbalance your back hand. As you perform the block, pull your forward hand back to your side in a chamber position (see figures 138 and 139).

Reach behind you with your blocking arm. Keep the elbow bent at a 90 degree angle. Pivot on the balls of your feet so that your hips and chest face opposite your back hand. (If your back hand is your right hand, for example, pivot so your chest and hips face the left.) This is to narrow the target area for the spear and to decrease the likelihood of serious injury should you be unable to block the spear.

Figure 138

Figure 139

Figure 140   **Figure 141**

As you pivot your body, twist your arm so that your elbow extends away from your body and your forearm faces up. This way, you block the spear and direct its course so that it slides by you. Once that has been accomplished, you can strike at the opponent, in order to force him to drop the weapon (see figures 140 and 141).

PRESSING BLOCKS

At the advanced level, attacking blocks, called pressing blocks, inflict damage on the attacker as well as blocking the attack. These blocks are intended to break bones and dislocate joints and should only be used in extreme circumstances where there is clear threat of bodily harm.

In general, you perform pressing blocks with your hands in the knife hand position. Your palms do most of the work. Essentially, one hand presses up on an object while the other hand presses down, or, depending on circumstances, one hand presses inward while the other presses outward. You can turn your hips or step into a pressing block in order to bring more power to the technique.

The goal is to break a bone, dislocate a joint, or break a weapon. You can also force an opponent to drop a weapon if you perform a pressing block on his arm while he holds the weapon. The block must be done quickly and powerfully to work.

When practicing, have a partner strike at you from different angles and experiment with different methods of performing the pressing block before you ever decide it could be useful to you in a confrontation (see figures 142 and 143 on the opposite page).

FOOT AND LEG BLOCKS

As you grow more skilled in Tae Kwon Do, you can use foot and leg blocks to stop an attacker. For example, simply lift your foot and push an attacker's leg away with it. Or lift your leg high, knee bent, as if you were chambering for a side kick. Use your leg to guard your side from a kick and then strike. Or use a crescent kick to block an opponent's punching arm.

Figure 142   **Figure 143**

Foot and leg blocks can be very useful because you don't need to get very close to your attacker to do them. However, they do require skill and practice in order to time them correctly. You have more room for error with other types of blocks. Remember, too, that you can combine foot and leg blocks with hand and arm blocks depending on the situation. If a strike slips past your guard, you may be able to block with your hand. Practice this with a partner to grow comfortable with the technique (see figures 144 and 145).

Figure 145   **Figure 146**

17

ADVANCED HAND STRIKING TECHNIQUES

Only a few hand strikes are introduced at the advanced level. The advanced practitioner is instead encouraged to master the techniques she has already learned and to add upper body power to her repertoire. In addition to using the techniques taught at the beginner and intermediate level, make a serious effort to use your whole body behind your hand strikes, to use the push/pull reciprocating method of striking, and to step into your techniques to add power, when this is appropriate. At the advanced level, in addition to watching yourself in the mirror and working with partners, you should use a striking post or heavy bag (preferably a heavy bag to prevent injuries). Striking a heavy bag using kicks and hand techniques gives you a chance to measure your power without actually having to hit other people as hard as you can. Use bag gloves or sparring equipment at first to prevent rolling your wrists on impact, which can cause sprains.

You can invest in a hanging heavy bag or a freestanding bag (See Part 2, Chapter 4 for further information about equipment) or check to see if your gym provides access to a heavy bag.

SPEAR HAND STRIKE

This strike, also called spear finger strike, is performed like straight punch, except your hand is in the spear hand position. This is the same as the knife hand position, with the exception that your first three fingertips should be even with each other (your middle finger will be slightly bent).

Unlike the knife hand strike, which uses the edge of your hand as the striking surface, the spear hand strike uses the tips of your fingers. To make sure

Figure 146

Figure 147

your fingers won't bend under impact, test your hand position by thrusting your fingers in the spear hand position against a wall.

Chamber your spear hand with your palm up near your waist. Keep your opposite hand a fist and extend it slightly in front of your body. Strike forward with your spear hand, while pulling back with your non-striking hand. Turn your spear hand palm down at the moment of impact and drive your fingertips into the target.

This technique is used mostly to strike at an opponent's midsection (in old martial arts movies, they use this technique to disembowel the enemy). It can also be used to strike to the throat (see figures 146 and 147).

SPEAR HAND THROAT GRAB

The spear hand strike can be used to grab an attacker's throat. The idea is to crush the larynx. To perform this strike, move your thumb away from the fingers, making a V shape. Thrust your hand forward to the opponent's throat, then grab it between you thumb and your hand and squeeze (see figure 148).

Figure 148

TWO-FINGER STRIKE

A variation of the spear hand uses the tips of the index and middle finger as the striking surface. Make a spear hand, then bend your two smallest fingers to your palm and cover them with your thumb. Bend your index and middle fingers to an angle slightly less than 90 degrees. These are your striking fingers. Chamber your hand at your side, palm up. Strike forward, your hand moving upward to the high section, turning your palm down at the moment of impact. Drive your two fingers into the target, the opponent's eyes. Remember to use your non-striking hand as a counterbalance (see figure 149).

Figure 149

UPSET (UPPER) PUNCH

The upset punch, sometimes called an upper punch, is similar to an uppercut a boxer uses. Chamber your fist palm down at your waist. From this position, punch forward and slightly upward, targeting the opponent's solar plexus or ribcage. At the moment of impact, twist your wrist so that your palm faces up. Your elbow should never be completely extended. Turn your body slightly and pull back with your non-punching hand to get more power behind your punch.

This technique can also target the high section, such as the opponent's jaw (see figures 150 and 151).

Figure 150

Figure 151

UPSET (UPPER) PUNCH, DOUBLE

In this technique, you perform upset punches with both hands simultaneously. Usually both hands strike to opposite sides of the same target area (for instance, to both sides of the rib cage or both sides of the jaw.) It is possible to punch with one hand to a middle target area and with the other hand to a different target area (see figures 152 and 153 on the following page).

Figure 152   **Figure 153**

BOXING SKILLS

Although most martial arts schools don't teach the techniques of boxing, acquiring boxing skills will help should you ever face a person who has basic fighting skills. You can practice boxing techniques on a heavy bag, in a shadow workout, or with a partner. By adding boxing skills to your repertoire of techniques, you'll make your other hand striking skills more powerful.

Boxing Stance

Begin with a good boxing stance. Keep one foot slightly more forward than the other, as in a fighting stance. Your body faces the opponent or the target. Turn your back shoulder slightly away so that your chest makes a smaller target and to generate more power when you punch with your back hand.

To get the most out of boxing techniques, you need to pivot on your feet. To avoid strikes, you need to move out of the way quickly. Thus, you should remain light on your feet until the moment you attack. While martial arts stances generally focus on strong, solid stances, the boxer's stance emphasizes agility and mobility. Only when a punch is thrown does the boxer dig into a stance in order to get her legs into the technique.

Make your hands into fists and keep them up, one hand on each side of your jaw to protect your head against a knockout punch. When you punch, your non-punching hand should remain up to protect your jaw at all times. After you strike, you should immediately return your striking hand to your jaw to protect your head. Think of returning your striking hand to your jaw faster than you delivered the blow in order to generate a snap to your strikes. This adds power and impact.

When you practice your boxing techniques, practice them in this stance, keeping your jaw guarded at all times (see figure 154). Then work on incorporating the different techniques into your martial arts sparring. For instance, in martial arts sparring if you leave your body unprotected (your hands up by your jaws), your opponent can win the match simply by scoring to your body a couple times. In boxing, punches to the body do not matter as much, since a knockout blow never lands on someone's midsection. That's also why the best fighters have sculpted abdomens — to take the punches to the body. Therefore, to practice only boxing methods when sparring is foolish. Instead, find ways to combine the techniques so that you can get the best of both worlds.

Figure 154

Jab

Use the jab to feel out your opponent and to distract her. It is never meant to be a debilitating blow. You might jab to the opponent's body to get her to drop her hands, then punch to the head.

Right handed boxers jab with their left hands. They use their right hands, which are more powerful, for power shots. As a martial artist, however, you should strive for balance, so you should practice jabs (and all punches) with both hands.

Jab with your forward hand. Instead of chambering your hand at your waist, as you do for martial arts techniques, keep your fist up near your jaw to protect your head. Then punch forward from your jaw, extending your elbow. Turn your body, pivoting on the balls of your feet, so that you shoulder goes into the punch (see figure 155).

Cross

The cross is similar to a reverse punch. A boxer typically uses her stronger arm for the

Figure 155

cross, but you should practice it with both arms. The back arm performs the cross. It almost invariably follows a jab or a sequence of jabs.

Keep your fist up. When you're ready to punch, drop your hand slightly so that your fist faces the target. Then strike forward. Extend your elbow while turning your upper body into the strike. Pivot on the balls of both feet as you strike, going in the direction of the punch. This adds the weight of your body behind the technique (see figure 156).

Hook

Boxers usually perform the hook with their forward hand, the same hand that performs the jab. A hook can be done using the back hand, which generates more power but makes the technique slower. Practice using both hands in both positions.

Cock your elbow to slightly less than a 90-degree angle. Raise your cocked arm parallel to the floor. Pivot on your feet into the direc-

Figure 156

tion of the punch, and twist your upper body into it. Your elbow should never straighten; it should always remain in the "hooked" position, even at the moment of impact. Lead with your shoulder instead of your hand or arm and you will perform the technique correctly (see figures 157 and 158).

Figure 157

Figure 158

Uppercut

The uppercut is similar to the upset punch, except that the uppercut is never done with both hands at the same time.

The uppercut is usually performed with the back hand. It moves in a semi-circular motion to strike the underside of the target area. Keep your non-punching fist chambered near your jaw. Then, lower your punching arm to waist level. Pivot as you strike upward with the punch. Extend your arm forward

Figure 159   **Figure 160**

and upward, palm facing you. Strike the target with the top of your knuckles (see figures 159 and 160).

Practicing Boxing Techniques

To get the most from your boxing techniqes, practice them in combinations. Punch several times in a row with your jab, then add a cross. Practice all of the techniques with both hands. Incorporate other aspects of boxing into your routine, such as punching a speed bag and practicing bob-and-weave avoidance techniques. The speed bag helps you learn to punch quickly in succession and to develop a punching rhythm. Practicing bob-and-weave, in which you duck and cover your head to avoid an opponent's strikes, can help you improve your sparring.

18

ADVANCED KICKING
TECHNIQUES

As practitioners build on the fundamentals at the advanced level, Tae Kwon Do kicking techniques become much more sophisticated. Most kicks at this level are not new; instead, they add elements to previously learned kicks. For example, the so-called tornado kick is really a reverse 360-degree axe kick. This means that you will add a jump and a reverse revolution to the axe kick in order to perform an impressive jumping-and-spinning technique.

The purpose of most advanced kicks is to challenge the martial artist and to teach her how to build on previously mastered techniques. The tornado kick is seldom used in sparring. A straightforward axe kick would probably be more effective in a street fight, since you would be more likely to perform the axe kick correctly and accurately. Nonetheless, advanced kicking techniques are spectacular to watch and exhilarating to master.

JUMP SPINNING WHEEL KICK

Once you've mastered the intermediate spinning wheel kick, you can add a jumping technique to it. To do so, stand in a back stance with your forward shoulder facing the target. Bend your knees and twist forward at the waist. From this position, jump, uncoiling as you go. As you jump, position your back leg (your kicking leg) in a spinning wheel position (leg extended, knee straight, foot tight). Think of springing into the target with your spinning wheel kick (see figures 161 and 162 on following page).

REVERSE KICKS

You can enhance almost all of the kicks you've previously learned by adding a reverse revolution. Although the reverse side kick is a beginner kick,

Figure 161   **Figure 162**

other reverse kicks are reserved until the advanced level. These include reverse crescent kicks (inside-to-outside, outside-to-inside and axe kicks) and reverse hooking kicks.

To perform this technique, face the target. Your back leg is your kicking leg. Simply lift your back leg into the chamber position and rotate to the rear 180 degrees. Strike with the kick (axe kick, hooking kick) as your back is to the target, then follow through and return to your starting position.

360-DEGREE KICKS

Almost any kick can be done as a 360-degree kick. This short-hand term means that you jump in the air and spin a complete 360-degree revolution, then kick, then return to your starting position. 360-degree kicks are almost always performed while revolving to the rear, in order to generate power and to make the execution of the kick smooth and strong.

Tornado Kick

To perform the tornado kick, which is a reverse 360-degree axe kick, face your target. Your front leg will be your kicking leg. In order to perform the revolution, twist your body so that your chest is coiled to the side. As you uncoil, push off into a jump. Lift your back leg and spin in reverse. As your back is turned to the target, lift your forward leg so that both feet are off the ground at the same time. Lift your forward leg up high. As you continue to spin so that you face the target, strike down with your forward foot, using your heel as the striking surface. This is the axe kick. Although this kick may seem impossible to successfully perform at first, all it requires is practice and speed. Practice the various parts slowly at first until you understand how they link together. Then move more and more quickly until you are able to perform the jump and the revolution with both feet off the ground at the same time (see figures 163, 164 and 165 on the following page).

Figure 163   **Figure 164**   **Figure 165**

360-Degree Reverse Roundhouse Kick

This technique is performed in the same way as the tornado kick. The only difference is that you use a roundhouse kick rather than an axe kick to strike the target.

360-Degree Reverse Side Kick

To perform this technique, you rotate to the front rather than to the rear. Face your target. Your forward leg will be your kicking leg. Thrust off your forward foot into a jump. Lift your back leg and spin forward. As you spin, lift your forward leg so that both feet are off the ground at the same time. As soon as your back is turned toward the target, chamber your forward leg and kick out as with a reverse kick. Practice moving quickly so that both feet are off the ground at the same time (see figures 166, 167 and 168).

Figure 166   **Figure 167**   **Figure 168**

PRACTICING ADVANCED KICKS

As you begin adding revolutions and jumps to your kicks, you will learn that you can modify all kicks to suit your interests, abilities and needs. Some martial artists enjoy jumping techniques and learn how to perform 540-degree and even 720-degree kicks. Some can jump high enough in the air that they can kick with both feet before returning to their starting position. While these kicks may not be realistic techniques to use in a street fight or even in sparring, they exercise the martial artist's abilities, skills and imagination, and should therefore be given an appropriate place in your martial arts practice session.

Women occasionally have difficulty with these types of kicks. We tend to be self-conscious, so practicing kicks that we know will cause us to fall on our heads can be nerve-wracking. Still, it is best to remember that if you aren't falling on your head on occasion, you're not trying hard enough.

We also have more of our weight centered in our hips, which can keep us more earth-bound than our brothers. As a whole, we tend to experiment less with what our bodies can do. All of these drawbacks can easily be countered if we simply practice and give ourselves permission to fail. Only through understanding what we're doing wrong can we learn to do it right.

Women do have the advantage of speed, and all of the advanced kicks rely on a combination of speed and timing — not brute force and breathtaking skill. Part 5, Chapter 21 discusses timing techniques for sparring; practicing these techniques improves your timing in all areas. Also, remember the jumping tips described in the intermediate section. Finally, a couple of "cheats" can help you learn the techniques and perform them accurately.

1.) Whenever you perform a revolution, always remember to twist at the waist. As you uncoil, you create the "spin" you need to complete a revolution (see figure 169).

2.) Lead with your shoulder, so that as you uncoil, you pull your rear shoulder back (or forward, depending on what direction you wish to go), propelling your spinning movement.

3.) Use footwork to make the revolution easier. For instance, as you face the target, your toes face the target. As you begin your spin, turn your foot so that your heel faces the target. Keep your heel up. This gives an extra torque to your lower body, so that

Figure 170

you can spring into your spin and complete the revolution correctly. If you need to generate even more spin, take a step forward before performing

Figure 170   **Figure 171**

your technique. As you step forward, place your foot so that your heel faces the target; then spin. You should eliminate this extra step as your technique improves (see figures 170 and 171).

These assists plus practice will help you master the revolving techniques so necessary to the advanced level of Tae Kwon Do training.

19
TAKEDOWNS, THROWS AND SWEEPS

Although Tae Kwon Do does not emphasize throws the way that other martial arts do, several throwing techniques are used. Women should take advantage of these throws since they can neutralize an opponent's size advantage. Women should also understand how throws are performed so they can defend against them. Any fight that goes to the ground is very dangerous for the victim.

To practice throws most effectively, you need a partner. Be certain your partner understands exactly what you plan to do so that he or she does not get hurt by the throw. Practice in a safe area, away from dangerous obstructions. Use padded mats to cushion your partner's fall. Never let go of your partner as you perform the technique. Help your partner all the way to the ground. (It should go without saying that you should not be this polite in a real fight.) By practicing prudently with the awareness that practicing these techniques can be dangerous, you should prevent any injuries.

Your partner shouldn't just fall down the moment you start the throwing technique. He or she should offer a realistic level of resistance, so that you can understand how much power and leverage you need to perform the techniques correctly. Nonetheless, you should tell your partner which direction he or she will be falling, and you should alert him or her when you're ready to begin the throw. You can do this by telling your partner, "Fall to the rear," and kihoping just before you start.

Let your partner practice the throwing techniques on you, too. Not only does this help you to see ways to improve your techniques, it helps you learn to defend against common throws.

LEARNING TO FALL

To prevent injuries, learn to fall correctly. Often, our instinct is to put a hand out to break a fall. This dangerous practice has led to more than one broken arm or sprained wrist. You should also avoid landing on your face or hitting your head.

To the Front

When falling to the front, lift your head and turn your face to the side. Thrust your free arm and shoulder forward, but don't put your hand directly on the ground to break the fall. To help prevent landing directly on your hand, keep your hand and arm moving forward, and bend your elbow as you fall. If you make a mistake or are forced to land directly on some part of your body, make it your shoulder and hip (see figure 172).

Figure 172

To the Back

When falling to the rear, don't stick your hand out to absorb the impact. Instead, absorb the blow on your hip and shoulder. Keep your chin tightly tucked into your chest at all times to prevent your head from striking the ground. As you fall, land first on your hip, roll slightly to your shoulder, then slap your hand, palm down, on the ground, extending your arm. This prevents you from continuing to roll and absorbs most of the impact of the fall (see figure 173).

Figure 173

PERFORMING THROWS, TAKEDOWNS AND SWEEPS

Most throwing techniques counter punches. Your opponent punches first, and then, using your opponent's punching hand or arm for leverage, you throw him or her. Since most confrontations at one point or another involve punches, this can be an effective countering technique. It can also convince an attacker not to escalate the confrontation any further.

Although these techniques can be used to counter a punch aimed at any target area, they're easiest to learn if you assume the attacker is punching toward your nose. Once you understand the techniques, have your partner attack to various parts of your body and adjust the technique to accommodate. Through continual practice, you will build trigger-fast responses so that in the case of a real threat, you can respond immediately.

SHOULDER TAKE DOWN

Step away from the opponent's punch, moving toward the opponent's body. Block the punch with your nearest hand and grab the opponent's wrist. With your free hand, grab the shoulder of the opponent's punching arm, and slide your closest foot forward, placing it behind the opponent's leg. Push against the shoulder while hooking your opponent's leg out from under with your own foot (see figures 174, 175 and 176).

Figure 174

Figure 175

Figure 176

When practicing with a partner, continue to hold his or her shoulder and wrist, helping your partner to the ground to avoid injury. In a real confrontation, you would release the opponent as soon as he or she loses balance and begins falling backward. The only exception would be if you planned to follow the throw with additional techniques, such as a punch to the face or a stomp to the solar plexus. Needless to say, using additional techniques on a fallen opponent is acceptable only if you're in serious physical danger.

HIP THROW

Block the opponent's punch with your outside arm while turning away from the punch. After you have turned, your back should face your opponent, and your feet should straddle the opponent's nearest foot. Reach behind you and grab the opponent's upper arm and shoulder. Untwist at the waist and pull the opponent forward against your hip. As the opponent loses balance, continue to pull and throw the opponent forward (see figures 177, 178 and 179).

Figure 177

Figure 178

Figure 179

To increase the effectiveness of this technique, try using a backward elbow strike to the opponent's solar plexus once you have blocked the punch and turned to straddle the opponent's foot. This distracts and disorients the opponent so that when you grab his or her arm and shoulder to throw, he or she will be less likely to resist the technique.

ANKLE SWEEP

Step away from the opponent's punch, moving toward his or her body. Grab the opponent's punching hand with your nearest hand. With your other hand, reach down, and sweeping in a circular motion, knock or pull the opponent's nearest forward ankle away, throwing him or her to the ground. This technique relies on speed and surprise, so practice it moving as quickly as you can (see figures 180 and 181).

Figure 180   **Figure 181**

THROWS COUNTERING KICKS

Although most takedown techniques are used to counter an opponent's punch, there is one kick that can be used against a roundhouse or spinning wheel technique. Keep in mind that countering a kick with a throw is more dangerous than countering a punch with a throw. A punch can be avoided or blocked and a takedown performed with little danger of physical harm. However, this is not true of takedowns countering kicks. You run the risk of getting kicked if you fail to do the technique perfectly. However, advanced practitioners should have enough skill.

Takedown techniques do not work against direct kicks such as front kicks and side kicks. It is dangerous to even attempt such a manuever.

Figure 182 **Figure 183**

Figure 184

Takedown Countering Roundhouse Kick or Spinning Wheel Kick

As your opponent performs the kick, slide in close and use both hands to stop and grab the kicking leg. As your opponent balances on one leg, slide your foot under his or her supporting leg and hook it out from under. In practice, make this technique less dangerous by grabbing your partner's shirt before hooking his or her leg out from under. In a fight, you can actually push against your opponent's chest to force him or her to lose balance (see figures 182, 183 and 184).

PRACTICING THROWS, TAKEDOWNS AND SWEEPS

As with other Tae Kwon Do techniques, the key to performing throws and is speed. The more quickly and decisively you move, the more likely your opponent will be caught off guard and unable to resist, and the more power you bring to the technique. Although you should practice techniques slowly and carefully at first, once you've gained confidence, move at full speed.

As you practice these techniques, you may think of other ways, perhaps better ways, to throw your opponents. This is part of being an advanced martial arts student. You may also need to modify the techniques to suit your abilities and physical attributes. For instance, a shorter woman might have difficulty performing the hip throw on taller men. She should think of different approaches she could take (grabbing the upper arm and wrist of the opponent, for example). If none of the modifications succeed, abandon the throw as not useful. There's nothing wrong with making this decision about what are essentially self-defense techniques since throws are illegal in sparring. Use only what works for you, avoid anything unnecessarily complicated, and modify the techniques to suit your particular circumstances.

PART FIVE:
DEVELOPING
FIGHTING SKILLS

20
STEP SPARRING

Step sparring, a method of practicing fighting techniques in combinations, helps prepare you for freestyle sparring or possible confrontations. Learning to hit others and being hit yourself can be difficult for women since few of us have much experience with contact sports, especially as adults. By following a series of carefully controlled and planned techniques, you can learn to master fighting techniques and will soon feel confident about your ability to withstand an attack.

WHAT IS STEP SPARRING?

Step sparring, which might also be called controlled sparring, is a method of practicing sparring techniques under special conditions so that you can learn without feeling overwhelmed or pressured by an actual sparring match. For this reason, beginning and intermediate martial artists find step sparring most useful, although even advanced fighters will want to use step sparring on occasion, particularly when incorporating new techniques into their sparring. Step sparring allows you to try out techniques not allowed in regular sparring matches.

STEP SPARRING BASICS

Beginning Tae Kwon Do practitioners should think of the art in defensive terms. Step sparring reinforces this concept, because at the basic level step sparring simply consists of blocks. The beginner blocks the attacker's kicks and punches, and retreats while saying, "I don't want to fight."

One partner attacks the other with one technique — a kick or a punch. The defending partner blocks the kick or punch using the appropriate technique (high block, low block, etc.) while saying, "I don't want to fight." As you move beyond basic step sparring, the defending partner will begin counterattacking the attacking partner.

Partners should always move quickly through step sparring because the purpose is to eliminate the element of thinking about what you're doing. This way, if you're attacked, instead of a paralyzing moment of "What should I do?" you will simply respond to the attack as you've been trained in step sparring. This prevents the attacker from gaining the upper hand in a confrontation.

Try combining different techniques to learn which go together most successfully. Advanced fighters should focus on developing combinations of techniques based on your specific skills and strengths.

Keep in mind that in step sparring, you're allowed to use techniques, such as knee and elbow strikes, that you cannot use in regular sparring.

FIGHTING RANGE

Step sparring helps you understand the theory of fighting range, which simply means that different techniques are suitable depending on the distance between you and your opponent. When the distance is so great that you can't kick or punch, you're outside of fighting range. It is possible that you could use a technique such as a flying sidekick or other jumping technique even when you're far away from your opponent, but generally these aren't used in sparring or in confrontations (see figure 185).

If you're just a few feet away, you're in kicking range. A kick will strike your opponent, but a hand technique will be too far away for effectiveness. When you're about 18 to 24 inches away from your opponent, you're in punching range. If you're slightly closer, you're in knee and elbow range. If you're only a few inches apart, you're again out of fighting range, since none of the techniques you could try would be effective (see figures 186, 187, 188 and 189).

Good fighters learn how to move into and out of the various fighting ranges in order to take advantage of the techniques they do well. When you practice step sparring, pay particular attention to fighting ranges. You will learn that once you kick, you are or can easily be in punching range, so it makes sense to put together combinations of techniques that start with a kick, continue with a punch and end with a knee or elbow strike.

You can use footwork techniques to move into and out of different fighting ranges. Use the patterns previously described (forward stepping, backward stepping, side stepping) and practice those that follow.

Figure 185

Figure 186

Figure 187

Figure 188

Figure 189

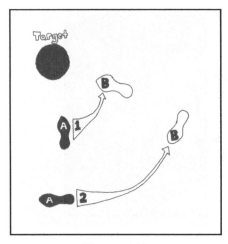

Figure 190

ANGLE STEPPING

Instead of moving in, out, or to the side, you can move at an angle (either forward or backward). This step helps you avoid an opponent's strike while remaining in range to strike yourself.

As the opponent kicks or punches, avoid the strike by sliding your forward foot at a 45-degree angle to your opponent (moving to the side opposite of the strike). Then slide your back foot into position and strike to your opponent's unguarded side.

You can move backward, away from the opponent (again at a 45-degree angle), to avoid a strike. Use this technique to move out of close range and into kicking range. In this case, move your back foot first, following with your forward foot. As you move you back foot, you can put your weight on that foot and kick with your forward foot to your opponent's unguarded side (see figure 190).

TRIANGLE STEPPING

Triangle stepping builds on angle stepping. While you can move in and out with angle stepping (simply following the same line back and forth), smarter opponents will catch on. To avoid this, move in a triangle instead of a straight line. That is, move in at a 45-degree angle. Then, as you move out, follow the opposite angle out so that you end several feet to the side of where you started.

Again, you can use a kick as you are stepping backward to prevent your opponent from attacking.

This technique can also be used if you

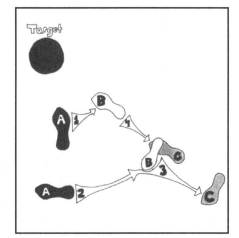

Figure 191

have used angle stepping to avoid a blow and discover that you need to move out of range quickly (see figure 191).

PRACTICING STEP SPARRING

Although step sparring requires a partner to be most effective, you can practice shadow step sparring by yourself. You can also use a heavy bag as an opponent if you want to practice your techniques full speed, at full force. Simply imagine that an opponent is kicking or punching, and respond.

Use care when working with partners. Never use full force against a partner. Limit contact to light touch, especially at first. Once you're more confident of your skills, you may wish to practice with heavier contact, but be certain your partner agrees and always listen if he or she asks you to lighten up. Wear sparring equipment if you want to use heavier contact. This can help prevent accidents from turning into injuries.

Step sparring follows a set approach so that both partners understand what is happening. This helps prevent injury. Beginning martial artists usually develop several sets of step sparring techniques that they practice, each one slightly different from the others and each one suitable for different circumstances. Before deciding on your sets, try different combinations and choose those that seem most effective. Always use more than one counterattacking technique, in case your first technique is ineffective against your opponent. Make sure your techniques flow smoothly. For example, a side kick can easily flow into a reverse kick, but a spinning wheel kick does not flow easily into a front kick. Kicks should come before punches and other close range striking techniques.

At the intermediate level, you'll have many different techniques to choose from, so take the time to create more sets of step sparring techniques, again trying different combinations before settling on those that seem most effective. Don't stop practicing your beginner step sparring sequences. Instead, practice all of your sets during your workouts.

At the advanced level, create an additional group of step sparring techniques incorporating your more advanced skills. Practice your beginning, intermediate and advanced step sparring sets whenever you work out. Occasionally, practice step sparring without using any of your set combinations. Instead, simply respond to an attack with whatever series of techniques comes to mind. This keeps your reactions quick and prevents practice from becoming stale.

STEP SPARRING SEQUENCE

Step sparring follows this sequence: the opponent attacks, and the defender blocks or evades the attack, then counters with a series of techniques. When the opponent (your partner) attacks, he or she should use a single technique. At the beginner level, the attacking partner should use a punch to the chest. As your skills improve, the attacking partner can choose different techniques to different target areas. This forces the defending partner to respond to a specific attack and to develop an arsenal of techniques that can be used against many different possible confrontations.

In the beginner stages of step sparring, the defending partner should respond to the attack (a punch) with a block. Begin with low blocks and high blocks. Once you're familiar with the routine, try additional blocks. As you become a more advanced martial artist, begin using footwork and body shifting to evade an attack, rather than directly blocking the technique. Evading an attack uses less energy than blocking a technique, and takes you out of the path of the opponent. By evading rather than blocking, you don't commit to a technique that could be used against you. Evading takes more skill than blocking, which is why you're in advanced training before you're capable of evading strikes without making a mistake. If you make a mistake when you block, chances are some portion of the attack will be deflected; if you make a mistake when you evade, you get the full force of your opponent's attack.

In sparring competition, blocking wastes time and commits you to a technique that cannot score a point, so once you're capable, it's good practice to slowly eliminate blocking from your step sparring techniques. Of course, in sparring competition, no matter what your level, you will continue to rely on blocks a great deal, but the more you work on evasion, the more skilled you become at fighting.

The point of blocking or evading the opponent's strike is to avoid getting struck — to avoid injury in a real confrontation, and to avoid losing points in a sparring match. You can often avoid a technique by starting one of your own immediately. For example, if an opponent starts a reverse kick, instead of blocking it, perform a reverse kick of your own. The opponent's kick will slide by you, and he or she will be open and unguarded when your kick strikes. This type of evasion requires correct timing. See Part 5, Chapter 21 for timing techniques.

When you're practicing step sparring, your partner should attack, and then stay in place as you block and counter. This helps prevent accidents, since your partner won't be moving in an unexpected direction.

Before you begin, both partners should signal their readiness by kihoping. When the defender is finished with her techniques, she should kihop again, this time to show she is done. The attacking partner should not return to the starting position until he or she hears this second kihop; accidents occur when the attacking partner thinks the defending partner is finished with her techniques and discovers that she is not. Take turns attacking and defending so that both partners gain experience.

CREATING STEP SPARRING ROUTINES

Create different step sparring routines to counter different kicks and punches to different target areas. Concentrate on the *type* of attack. Instead of having one step sparring routine for side kicks and one for reverse side kicks, realize that you can respond to both techniques in the same way. Through practice, you can determine the types of techniques that belong in each group and develop a step sparring routine to respond to that group of techniques. Remember that you'll have to block and move differently depending on whether the attack is coming to your left or your right, and practice the routine both ways. For instance, if you respond to a punch to your left side by low blocking with your left hand and performing a front kick with your right leg, practice blocking a punch to your right side by low blocking with your right hand and performing a front kick with your left leg.

Although it is helpful to have set routines, don't forget to invent step sparring routines sometimes. Simply respond to your partner's attack with a set of just-thought-up techniques. This helps keep your step sparring fresh, and helps you learn what to do if you freeze during a confrontation. Also, it reminds you that some combinations don't work well together. You and your partner can analyze your success at inventing step sparring routines on the spur of the moment and come up with strategies for improving this part of your training.

PRACTICE DRILLS

Use the following step sparring routines to get started. Once you've practiced them a few times and understand the process, create your own sets of techniques to memorize and practice. For these drills, the attacking partner starts in a front stance with her left leg forward. She should perform a low block, then kihop. The defending partner should stand naturally and kihop after the attacking partner signals readiness. Once the attacking partner hears the defender's kihop, she is free to attack at anytime by stepping forward with her right leg and at the same time punching to the defender's chest with her right hand (see figure 190).

Figure 190

Once you've practiced and understand the following drills, change the attack sequence. Have the attacking partner start with her right leg forward and use a kick; any stance and any technique can be used.

Counter with Punch

To avoid the punch, side step to the right. Block the punch with your left hand. Punch to your partner's ribs with your right hand(see figures 191 and 192 on the following page).

Variations:

You can vary this counter by adding an additional punch with your left hand or by punching twice with your right hand. The punches can also be directed at your partner's head.

Figure 191   **Figure 192**

Counter with Elbow Strike

As your partner punches, perform a block with your left arm. As you block, step forward and deliver an elbow strike to the head with your right arm. Kihop to signal the end of the sequence (see figures 193 and 194).

Variation:

You can vary this technique by performing a double elbow strike. Strike with your right elbow then twist at the waist and strike with your left elbow.

Counter with Roundhouse Kick

To avoid the punch, sidestep to the left, away from your partner. Perform a roundhouse kick with your right leg (see figures 195 and 196).

Variation:

Punch one or more times to the side of your partner's ribs. To disable an attacker, punch to the kidneys (see figure 197).

Counter with Front Kick

To avoid the punch, side step to the right. Block the punch with your left hand. Perform a front kick to the groin or midsection (see figures 198 and 199 on the following page).

Variation:

Add a second front kick, this one to the head. Don't set your kicking leg down between kicks.

Figure 193

Figure 194

Figure 195

Figure 196

Figure 197

Figure 198

Figure 199

Figure 200

Variation:

Add a punch to the midsection or the head after the front kick (see figure 200).

Counter with Side Kick

To avoid the punch, side step to the left and block the punch with your right hand. Perform a side kick to your partner's ribs, using either leg (see figures 201 and 202 on the following page).

Variation:

Add a reverse kick after you complete the sidekick.

Variation:

Add a reverse punch after you kick, putting your kicking foot in closer to the attacking partner and using your non-punching arm to guard.

Figure 201   Figure 202

Crescent Kick Block with Hooking Kick Counter

To avoid the punch, step back slightly with your left leg, then perform an inside-to-outside crescent kick with your left leg. Use this kick to knock your partner's hand away. As you return your left leg to its starting position, perform a hooking kick to the head with your right leg (see figures 203 and 204).

Figure 203   Figure 204

Figure 205

Variation:

After you complete the hooking kick, perform a roundhouse kick with the same leg (don't set your leg down between kicks.) See figure 205.

Variation:

Use a sidekick to the midsection instead of the hooking kick.

Counter with Palm Strike and Knee Strike

Use a high block with your left hand to block the punch. Then perform a palm strike to your partner's nose with your right hand. Grab your partner's neck and pull her head toward your knee. Perform a knee strike to your partner's face (see figures 206, 207 and 208).

Figure 206

Figure 207

Figure 208

21
FREESTYLE SPARRING

Like step sparring, freestyle sparring is a method of practicing techniques under controlled conditions. The difference is that each partner continually attacks and defends in freestyle sparring.

Although step sparring helps you learn new techniques, counters and defensive manuevers, you must actually fight in freestyle sparring matches to become a proficient martial artist.

In freestyle sparring, you perform different techniques against an opponent, with the intention of scoring a point. Partners move back and forth (usually within a circumscribed area called "the ring") exchanging techniques and trying to block, avoid and counter one another's movements.

Freestyle sparring is not intended to mimic a street fight or confrontation. Instead, it is a means for you to practice your techniques, to learn about timing and to face opponents of various sizes and skill levels. Although you never know what might happen in a street fight, freestyle sparring practice can help you prepare for such an event. So do other elements of martial arts practice, such as self-defense training, step sparring routines, and the simple repetitive practice of your techniques.

GETTING HIT

For most women, the hardest part of sparring isn't using difficult techniques or scoring points or defending against kicks to the head. The hardest part of sparring is getting hit. Less difficult, but still challenging, is actually hitting other people. Men often participate in contact sports throughout their lives, but many women don't. We're not accustomed to getting hit and can find the process intimidating.

First, realize that becoming comfortable with physical contact is simply a matter of practice. Men tend to be more physical beings than women; they punch their buddies, roughhouse with their kids, play basketball hard and if they don't come home with bruises, they're disappointed. Women hug their friends, kiss their kids, and work out on treadmills. Of course getting kicked in the head is disorienting the first time or two.

Second, practice with sensitive partners — people who are willing to slow down, to use very light contact (if any), and to listen to you and offer encouragement.

Third, and finally, practice your techniques so that you're hitting something, whether it's a heavy bag or a target you rig up yourself. Getting accustomed to contact requires practice, and you should obtain that practice any way you can.

PROTECTIVE EQUIPMENT

Protective equipment, called sparring gear, consists of padded protectors that keep you and your sparring partner from getting bruised (see figure 209). Sparring gear protects against accidental injury and miscalculated techniques. Equipment should be used in every sparring match, but it's especially important when you're sparring people you're unfamiliar with and when you're using new techniques.

Many different pieces of protective gear exist. What you should use depends on the type of sparring you do (ITF fighters use less equipment than WTF fighters), how much contact you have while sparring, what your regular partners prefer, and what your instructor (if any) recommends. In addition, tournament organizers may require certain pieces of protective gear, so

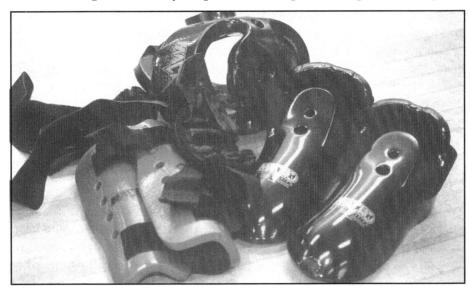

Figure 209

whether you use it on a regular basis, you should have it on hand.

Headgear protects the sides and back of your head. Some pieces come with a removable mask to protect your face. Headgear can feel heavy and can interfere with your vision, so try before you buy. Since kicks to the head are common in Tae Kwon Do, headgear is strongly recommended. (Required in some tournament competitions). *Mouthguards* protect your teeth and your mouth. They're inexpensive, easy to use, and highly recommended. (Required in some tournament competitions.) *Chest protectors* cover your chest and ribs. If you spar WTF-style or use heavy contact, chest protectors are highly recommended (Required in WTF-style competition.) *Groin protectors* protect the groin. (Required for men in all tournament competitions.) *Forearm guards* protect the forearms from bumps and bruises. They can interfere with techniques, although some users swear by them. (Not required.) *Hand protectors* protect your partner from hand techniques that land too hard. Suppliers sell several types. The most common type, made of padded cotton or plastic-covered foam, covers the entire hand, strapping around the wrist. The less common glove-style protector, usually made of leather, looks like a fingerless glove with padding. This type of hand protector can also be used for bag work but may not be accepted at all tournaments. (Required in some tournament competitions.) *Shin guards* protect your shins from bumps and bruises. If you spar with medium or heavy contact, these are a must. If you use your legs to block kicks, you should invest in shin guards. (Not required.) *Foot protectors* protect your partner in case you kick too hard. Several types exist. One type slides onto the foot and covers the instep of the foot. Another type combines a shin guard with a foot protector all in one piece. WTF-style fighters prefer this kind. They protect well against roundhouse kicks, but not against kicks that use the heel of the foot. Another type of protector covers the entire foot, including the toes, the heel and the sides of the foot. It attaches with a strap that wraps around the bottom of the foot. This type is preferred by ITF-style fighters, who use their heels to perform crescent kicks and spining wheel kicks. It is slightly heavier and more cumbersome than the other styles. (Required at some tournament competitions.)

TARGET AREAS

In Tae Kwon Do sparring, you can only strike to certain target areas. This restriction is meant to prevent injury to your partner. The target areas include the sides of the head, but not the nose and throat, and not the back or the top of the head. The chest, including the ribs and the sides of the chest, is a legal target area. The back is not a legal target area, nor are the legs, and especially not the groin and knees. Any technique that lands below the belt is illegal. Elbow and knee strikes are not allowed, nor are takedowns, sweeps and throws.

In general, hand techniques are not allowed to the head. This means punches must be targeted to the chest. For the most part, hand techniques are limited to punches, but in some cases, advanced fighters will be able to use any hand technique to the body.

When sparring informally with partners, you can agree to any set of rules you like, but most Tae Kwon Do fighters prefer to practice according to tournament rules. This is so they practice using techniques, strategies and tactics that will succeed in tournament.

POINT SCORING

In competition, you win the match by landing the most unblocked strikes on your opponent. Different styles count points differently. In Olympic-style Tae Kwon Do, only strikes that cause a trembling blow when they land count for a point. The strike must land, unblocked, and move the defender visibly through space for a point to be awarded. For this reason, Olympic-style Tae Kwon Do (also known as WTF-style) favors powerful back leg kicks (such as the back leg roundhouse kick) and uses fewer punches. Contact is generally heavier, and fighters use more equipment to protect themselves.

In traditional Tae Kwon Do (ITF-style), judges use a traditional point system. The fighter's technique, accuracy and control count more than power. A perfect technique, even if partially blocked, can sometimes count for a point. In most cases, hand techniques to the head are illegal, and kicks to the head count as two points since they require superior technique than kicks to the body. Kicks and punches to the body count for one point. In this type of sparring, your control (the ability to strike a target without damaging it) is of greatest importance.

Official matches usually last two minutes. The fighter who accumulates the most points wins the match.

Occasionally, a tournament sponsor will specify exceptions to these general rules. If you're interested in participating in a tournament, request the tournament rules and study them, then practice for the specific rules of the tournament. Although tournament rules vary, it makes sense to practice freestyle sparring according to basic, accepted guidelines. For your own development as a martial artist, you should make occasional exceptions to these rules, but make certain you and your partners agree to abide by whatever rules you set.

COURTESY IN SPARRING

The tenet of courtesy requires you to spar using only those techniques your partner has learned. If you're an intermediate practitioner and you spar a beginner, do not overwhelm her with your hooking kicks. Instead, limit yourself to those techniques that she knows so that she's prepared for the possibilities and can respond appropriately. If a partner does not know how to perform a hooking kick, and you use one in sparring, she will not expect it and will not understand how it works. Therefore, she might block it incorrectly, evade it the wrong way, or otherwise make a mistake that could lead to injury. Only use superior techniques if your partner doesn't mind and would like the challenge of sparring against techniques she does not know. Never do this at the beginner level; it is only appropriate at the intermediate level and above.

During practice sparring, it is courteous to acknowledge any points your partner scores. This can be done by nodding your head, saying "point," or tapping the target area where the point scored. This informal system allows partners to assess how they're doing and learn which techniques are effective.

SPARRING WITHOUT PARTNERS

Although freestyle sparring requires a partner, you can work on techniques, footwork and bodyshifting even without one. You can shadow spar, watching yourself in a mirror, or you can spar a heavy bag, which is about the weight and size of a real person. Both shadow sparring and sparring a heavy bag allow you the opportunity to work on offensive techniques, but to become a good fighter, you do need to spar good fighters. Even if you spar some fighters who aren't at your skill level, you can still learn something from every partner you spar with.

SPARRING BASICS

Beginning fighters often spar very far away from each other in order to avoid contact, which can be a little scary, and because they don't have confidence in their control. When they realize the problem, they sometimes go to the opposite extreme, sparring so close to each other that no techniques can be used effectively. Learn fighting range by step sparring and put this knowledge to use in freestyle sparring. Go slowly, but try to make light contact with your partner in order to build your confidence.

To begin a sparring match, agree to a time limit and a ring size. As a courtesy, bow to your partner and to any instructor or senior belt watching. Assume a fighting stance. When you're ready, wait for the signal. The senior partner (or the instructor) shouts, "Sijak" or "Begin." Kihop to show your partner you're ready, then begin sparring.

To stop the match at any time, so that you can fix a piece of equipment or because you sprained your ankle, hold up your hands, yell "time" or "stop," and step away from your partner. Don't turn your back. If your partner hasn't heard you, you could get hurt. In an official match, stepping out like this is an automatic forfeit, but there is no need to be so formal in practice sparring. In an official match, if your equipment comes loose or you're injured, the judges will stop the match and allow you the opportunity to fix your equipment or assess your injury. This will not automatically disqualify you.

Watch your partner's eyes at all times as you spar. This gives you clues as to what she plans to do next. Besides, if you're watching her left leg, you won't see the right punch coming. Keep your eyes up and your mind focused on the match at all times.

TIMING TECHNIQUES

The best way to improve your sparring performance is simply to practice sparring. However, some drills, called timing techniques, can enhance your skills, quicken your reflexes and improve your sparring. Timing techniques help you to see openings in your partner's guard and to strike immediately. Not only do these drills help you see the openings, they help you *anticipate* the openings.

Understanding Timing Techniques

To understand timing techniques, you have to understand that each fighting technique has inherent strengths and weaknesses. As a fighter, you hope to exploit the technique's weaknesses when you're defending and to use its strengths when you're attacking.

For example, the roundhouse kick is an excellent technique for scoring high. Even people with limited flexibility can kick head high with a roundhouse kick. It can also be very fast, and therefore hard to block or avoid. Its weakness, however, is that it can leave your chest open and unguarded when you perform it. A good opponent will spot this and immediately strike to your chest.

If you've been practicing timing techniques, you know this weakness. Therefore, if your partner uses a roundhouse kick, you'll move immediately to exploit its weakness. And, since you understand this weakness, you'll attempt to compensate for it when you use the technique yourself. For instance, you can practice performing roundhouse kicks with both hands guarding your chest.

Ideally, you should work with a partner to hone your skills, but you can practice timing techniques on a heavy bag or in front of a mirror.

Practice the following drills, then devise your own depending on the techniques you use. All of the drills listed below follow a similar sequence, which you can vary as you grow more comfortable with the drills.

Partners assume fighting stances and both kihop to show when they're ready. The attacking partner attacks with one technique. The defending partner should block and/or counter the technique, moving quickly and smoothly. She should kihop when she is finished. Both partners should then return to the beginning position. Partners should take turns attacking and defending.

BLOCKING AND COUNTERING DRILLS

Beginning fighters should block their opponent's techniques to avoid the attack and to prevent your opponent from scoring. Then launch your own attack, which is called the counter or counterattack. In the beginning stages, keep these counterattacks simple. Use more sophisticated counters as you grow more skilled.

Blocking and Countering Punches

Partners assume fighting stances facing the same direction. The attacking partner punches to your midsection with his or her forward hand. Block this punch with any of the block you have learned. Practice until you are comfortable deflecting your partner's hand away. Then add the countering technique: a reverse punch to your partner's midsection (remember, a reverse punch uses your back hand.) Step into the punch if you need to close distance. You need to time this technique so that you launch your punch just as you are deflecting the block; this leaves your partner's chest open for your strike. You can add another punch with your forward hand if your partner's midsection remains unguarded (see figures 210, 211 and 212).

Figure 210

Figure 211

Figure 212

| Figure 213 | Figure 214 |

Blocking and Countering Side Kicks

Partners assume fighting stances facing the same direction. The attacking partner performs a sidekick with his or her forward leg. Use a low block to sweep the leg out of the way (use your forward hand). Remember to block down over your leg. Practice this technique several times before adding the countering technique, a punch. To do this, sweep your partner's leg aside and quickly step forward and punch. By practicing this technique repeatedly, you will learn to spot a sidekick, and you'll be able to block and counter it before your opponent can strike (see figures 213 and 214).

Variation: Blocking and Countering Front Kicks

Use the same drill as for countering the sidekick, but instead of sweeping the attacking partner's leg aside, block directly downward on the front kick to move your partner's leg out of the way. Follow with a counterattack.

Blocking and Countering Crescent Kicks

Assume fighting stances. The attacking partner performs a crescent kick (using either leg and moving either outside-to-inside or inside-to-outside). Block the kick with a high block. Instead of pushing the kick aside, however, keep the kick blocked. Practice this technique until you're comfortable with it. Then step in and add a punch (see figures 215 and 216).

Depending on which leg your partner uses and which direction the kick comes at you, you will use a different arm to block the kick. This requires extra practice, so that you can identify the precise kick your partner is performing before attempting to block and counter it.

Figure 215

Figure 216

Figure 217

Figure 218

Blocking and Countering Reverse Kicks

Assume fighting stances, partners' chests facing in opposite directions. The attacking partner performs a reverse kick. With your forward arm, use a low block to push the kick aside. Push or sweep in the same direction your partner is already rotating, using her momentum against her. Once you are consistently able to block the reverse kick out of the way, add a counter by stepping in and punching to the middle section (see figures 217 and 218).

Variation: Blocking and Countering Other Kicks

The side kick, crescent kick and reverse kick drills work for all different kinds of kicks. Modify them slightly to suit your needs, and practice blocking and countering different kicks. For instance, the side kick drill can also work on roundhouse kicks (partners should face opposite directions). Experiment to

Figure 219

Figure 220

learn what works best for you, then practice these timing techniques during each workout.

COUNTERING STRIKES WITHOUT BLOCKING

As you grow more skilled and practice your timing techniques, you'll no longer block an attack before countering. Blocking takes time and commits you to a technique that cannot score a point. In sparring, where every second counts, this is a drawback. (Of course, in every sparring match you'll have to block attacks, but the more often you can avoid it, the better your sparring will be.) Instead of blocking, use footwork and body shifting to avoid a technique and then counter with one of your own attacks. The following techniques will get you started.

Countering a Punch

Partners should assume fighting stances facing the same way. The attacking partner performs a reverse punch. Step to the side, away from the punch, and strike to the opponent's midsection (see figure 219). You may need to step forward to get into range. You can also use angle stepping to avoid the punch *and* get into range or, you can use a kick instead of trying to move into punching range (see figure 220).

Countering a Side Kick

Partners assume fighting stances facing the same way. The attacking partner performs a side kick with her forward leg. Instead of blocking the kick, step away from the strike while moving toward your partner's body and strike to the middle section.

Variation:

This technique can be used against any kick. The only difference is that you will move in different directions depending on what leg your attacking partner uses and what type of kick she performs. Practice countering different kicks in this way so often that you can automatically sense the direction of the kick and step away from it before it strikes.

COUNTERING WITH KICKS

Basic timing techniques require you put to use much of what you've learned about footwork and speed. You learn to determine the type of technique your partner is using before he or she strikes. As your skill grows, you can block or counter these techniques more consistently. As you move into intermediate timing drills, you learn to counter your partner's techniques using kicks without blocking or stepping to the side to avoid an attack. Countering with a kick still leaves you in kicking range, where you're less vulnerable. Also, in competition judges are more likely to notice and score kicking techniques than they are hand techniques, so it is wise to rely on your kicking techniques as much as possible. Using a kick to counter a strike is faster as well. You can perform your kick — your counterattack — even before your partner has finished striking.

Countering with Reverse Kicks

Against a side kick

Assume fighting stances facing opposite directions. The attacking partner performs a sidekick using his or her front leg. As soon as your partner chambers his or her leg for the kick, immediately turn and perform a reverse kick to your partner's midsection. Don't try to block the kick first and then perform your own kick. By turning to do the reverse kick, you will avoid your partner's kick and can take advantage of the opening that will follow. Also, be aware of your body positions. If you and your partner are facing the same direction, this timing technique will not work. This problem can be overcome with some imagination, for instance, by using a different timing technique or by shifting your feet before you launch the kick. You can also add a punch after the reverse kick to increase your chances of scoring (see figures 221 and 222 on the following page).

Against a reverse kick

Assume fighting stances facing in opposite directions. The attacking partner performs a reverse kick. As soon as you see your partner chamber her leg, turn and perform a reverse kick. You can also add a reverse punch.

Figure 221

Figure 222

Against a roundhouse kick

Assume fighting stances facing in opposite directions. The attacking partner performs a roundhouse kick with her back leg. As soon as you see your partner chamber her leg, perform a reverse kick.

Against a spinning wheel kick

Assume fighting stances facing opposite directions. The attacking partner performs a spinning wheel kick. As soon as you see her begin the kick, perform a reverse kick. Lean over your supporting foot to avoid your opponent's spinning wheel kick.

Countering with Spinning Wheel Kicks

Spinning wheel kicks can also be used to counter almost any kicking technique. Use them exactly as you would a reverse kick. Each of the above drills can be performed with a spinning wheel kick. Simply substitute a spinning wheel kick for the reverse kick.

ADVANCED TIMING DRILLS

The drills described above help beginning and intermediate fighters improve their sparring effectiveness. You can create additional drills using countering techniques of your choice. But to truly improve your timing skills at the advanced level, both partners should work on their timing skills at the same time. For example, your opponent performs a reverse kick. Using your knowledge of timing techniques, you would counter by performing a reverse kick. But because your partner also understands timing techniques, she would perform a reverse kick to counter your reverse kick. In essence, she would perform two reverse kicks in a row. Perhaps you see her second reverse kick coming, and instead of doing a second reverse kick of your own, you step forward and punch.

Figure 223

Figure 224

Figure 225

At the advanced level, having both partners practice timing techniques at the same time is a good habit. Also, vary the types of timing techniques you do. Don't always step to the side and perform a punch. Sometimes, use a reverse kick instead. Put together different drills, adding variations as you grow more skilled (see figures 223, 224 and 225).

EXTENDED COMBINATION DRILL

Try not to fall into predictable routines. Often, a fighter will rely mostly on sidekicks, or will counter every reverse kick with a punch. In addition, fighters frequently perform one technique and then stop. However, adding variety to your sparring makes you a better fighter, and using more than one or two techniques in a row is an excellent strategy. This can overwhelm your opponent, causing her to lower her guard.

One way to add variety to your sparring and to practice using more than one technique at a time is the extended combination drill. In this drill, you perform a series of techniques while your partner blocks the strikes or steps backward as you move forward. Practicing this drill also improves your understanding of how techniques work together.

To do it, both partners assume fighting stances and kihop to indicate their readiness. Then perform two techniques of any kind, kihoping when you're finished. Next, your partner performs two techniques as you block them or move backward out of the way. She should also kihop to show that she's done. Then perform three techniques (use different ones from those you performed in the first series), kihop, and allow your partner to perform three techniques. Continue adding one technique each turn until you're performing six to eight techniques in a row. Assess your performance, deciding which techniques worked best together.

Variation:

As your skills increase, do the combination drill faster. Have someone time each partner's set of techniques. Agree to do the same number of techniques per series. Try to beat your partner's time.

Variation:

Have the defending partner call out a number between two and eight. This is the number of techniques the attacking partner must do in her next series.

Variation:

If you don't have a partner available, the combination drill can be done without a partner. Simply work on quickly stringing together several techniques. You can use a heavy bag or do the drill as a shadow drill.

SPARRING BIGGER PEOPLE

Women should always spar male partners when they have the chance, since in a confrontation you're more likely to have to defend yourself against a man. In addition, men are generally taller and heavier than women, so you have to fight them differently. It is extremely important to understand how to modify your techniques and sparring habits to suit the opponent you face.

Don't let someone else's size intimidate you. Stay focused. Think only of sparring to the best of your ability.

In order to get the most from your sparring efforts, take an honest inventory of your body type. Are you shorter than most of the people you spar? Are you heavier or lighter than most other women? Keep in mind that speed counters mass, so even if you're smaller than your opponent, you can be faster, and therefore just as powerful. If you're lighter in weight and have less muscle mass, you can be more flexible, which means that your kicks can be higher and faster.

For many women, fighting in close (within punching range) works well. It neutralizes the bigger person's height advantage. In-close fighting can be used successfully against people who like to counter defensively, especially since they rely primarily on kicks as counters. If you're in punching range, it's more difficult for them to counter your techniques. Because Tae Kwon Do is perceived as a kicking art, it rarely occurs to practitioners how effective it can be to fight inside.

You can use kicks to manuever into and out of punching range. One way to do this is to feint with a kick. Then, instead of returning your foot to its original position, drop it right in front of your opponent. Now you're in punching range, so you can slide or step in with a punch. The feinted kick covers you as you move in and distracts your partner. Before your opponent counters or starts trading punches with you, move out of sparring range with another kick.

Develop a good middle kick, perhaps a front kick, and a good high kick, perhaps a roundhouse kick. Feint with these to move into punching range. Then execute a quick series of hand techniques, either middle or high (or both), depending on the openings you see. Finally, use a middle kick, such as a front kick, to push back out of punching range. Moving out of punching range requires the use of a bail-out technique. These are always good to have on hand for whenever you get into trouble. A tightly chambered reverse kick, a middle front kick or a spinning backfist all work well. Once out of punching range, get ready to move in again. The key to this kind of sparring is moving in and out as quickly as possible. This keeps you in control of the match and helps you capitalize on your strengths and minimize your weaknesses.

A good sidekick will keep opponents from moving inside on you. If the sidekick alone doesn't do the trick, follow it up with a reverse kick. A reverse kick can also be used to move back out of punching range.

Many female martial artists find themselves frustrated when they kick their sparring opponent and essentially bounce off him. Practice is the best way to prevent this recoiling of energy, which is a problem not limited to women, but since we're smaller, it does happen to us more.

When you kick full power against a heavy, inflexible target, especially with a technique that's new to you, your body can't account for the sudden energy of the strike, so the energy recoils back on you and you bounce off your target. This only happens when your target doesn't absorb some of the energy, such as by stepping back. To solve this problem, practice doing full contact techniques. Learn to control the kick, redistribute your weight, and maintain your balance while focusing your energy on the target. If you do the technique correctly, the target (your opponent) will absorb most, if not all, of your energy. Heavy bag training is a necessity for this. You can kick it pretty hard and it won't move, just like some people. Plus, the heavy bag never lies. If you're off target, you'll know it. If you're too high or too low, you'll know it. You'll probably fall down, which is how you'll know it. To kick the heavy bag so that the blow is powerful enough to move *it* instead of *you*, you must hit it accurately, and you must hit it hard, transferring your energy to it. If you master this, you'll rarely find yourself bouncing off partners during sparring. Of course, you would never kick your partner as hard as you kick the heavy bag!

By following these techniques and modifying them to suit your needs, you can successfully spar taller, heavier opponents.

KICKING VARIETY

Women who develop a strong repertoire of kicks have a significant advantage in sparring. Many martial artists rely on just a few kicks (the roundhouse kick, side kick and reverse kick seem to be the favorites). This can be a weakness. Since women generally have speed, flexibility and agility, you should be able to add almost any kick to your sparring arsenal. Don't neglect the front kick, the crescent (or axe) kick, reverse crescent kick and hooking kick. Don't forget double kicks. Use combination drills to help you learn how to add new kicks to your sparring.

MENTAL PREPARATION

In order to become the most accomplished martial artist possible, keep an open mind. Watch other fighters and learn from them. Spar different partners and discuss your performance. Videotape your matches to see what tendencies crop up. Watch competitions to see what advanced fighters do. Read instructional articles and books and watch how-to videos. Most of all, practice on your own.

Much of sparring is mental preparation rather than physical exertion. If you have confidence, you're more likely to react quickly and without hesitation. If you're unsure, you may let opportunities to score pass you by. At first, it can be difficult to develop confidence, since you don't know what you're doing most of the time. That's why practicing timing techniques and combination drills is crucial. These drills help you spar with confidence.

Although you may get discouraged or frustrated when you spar, you must stay focused and continue to fight confidently. If you let your doubts influence you, your opponent will have won the match without scoring a point. Realize that even a bad sparring match helps you learn and grow.

To keep from getting distracted, concern yourself only with what you're doing. Are you taking advantage of openings that come up? Are you anticipating your opponent's attacks? Are you getting faster, stronger, smarter? Don't worry about how you compare to your opponent or to other martial artists. Learn to be the best martial artist you can be.

SIZE UP YOUR OPPONENT

Analyze how you spar different fighters. Tall people, short people, heavy contact fighters, light contact fighters — all require a slightly different approach. If one opponent relies on a fast-paced, aggressive attack, your approach should be different from when you face a fighter who relies primarily on defensive countering techniques. Your opponents should not dictate the match, but you should respond to each indivdual as just that — an individual. If one person never gets out of the way of your axe kick, by all means keep it coming. If another opponent easily evades it and counterattacks successfully, find another approach. Sparring different people differently forces you to add variety to your sparring, which is essential to proficiency in Tae Kwon Do.

Think of sparring as a work in progress, not a final product. It should change, grow, mature and adjust as you learn.

PART SIX:
SELF-DEFENSE TECHNIQUES

22
PHILOSOPHY OF
SELF-DEFENSE

Tae Kwon Do is a defensive art. Practitioners should never use the techniques to initiate an attack, only to defend themselves. Your defense and counterattack should suit the situation at hand. That means breaking someone's arm because he looked at you funny is inappropriate to the spirit of Tae Kwon Do.

The best self-defense tactic possible is simply to avoid a fight. Leave if you feel a confrontation might be brewing. Because fights can escalate dangerously, it is best to avoid them entirely. What exactly are you going to do when your opponent pulls out a double-barrel shotgun?

LEVELS OF SELF-DEFENSE

However, there may be times when you cannot avoid a confrontation. If this happens, Tae Kwon Do practitioners have three levels of response to draw from. The first response, escape, is fairly straightforward. You leave the scene before anything happens. Or suppose your attacker grabs your arm. You simply pull your arm free and then leave. This is the least dramatic type of self-defense, but it is the most successful. You communicate to your assailant that you don't intend to be messed with, but you don't escalate the situation by over-reacting.

The second level is control. At this level, you perform a self-defense technique that allows you to "control" the attacker without causing physical harm. Use this level when an attacker persists. If, for instance, you say, "I don't want to fight," and the attacker grabs your shoulder, you might do a self-defense technique to escape. If he then threatened you again before you could leave the scene, or if he grabbed your shoulder a second time, you would move to the control level. At this level, you have more direct contact with your assailant, but you do nothing to cause lasting injury. Instead, you rely on traps, holds and locks to stop the attacker, inflict minor temporary pain and end the attack.

The third level is retaliation or counterattack. In this case, your intention is to cause your attacker harm. You will gain control of the attacker and then strike him in order to convince him to stop, or, if necessary, render him unable to continue his attack.

FINISH THE FIGHT

Of course, sometimes you might underestimate the seriousness of an attacker. For this reason, you must always be prepared to finish the fight — that is, to render the attacker unable to continue. If for any reason you are unwilling to do so, you must be prepared to accept the consequences of this decision — which might be your physical endangerment. If you engage in a fight, you must accept that you could seriously injure your opponent or that you might be unable to defend yourself. The concept of "finishing the fight" means that once you've committed to a physical confrontation, you're committed to ending it, however that might turn out. This is serious indeed. Don't go this road if you can ever walk away.

SELF-DEFENSE AGAINST KNOWN ATTACKERS

Women must realize that the threat of physical harm doesn't come simply from random strangers, but instead from people you know and trust. For this reason, you should understand the escape and control techniques. After all, if it's your boyfriend (soon to be ex-boyfriend) who is hitting you, do you really want to gouge his eyes out with your car keys? Even if you're in physical danger, it can be extremely difficult to overcome your relationship with someone long enough to put him in the hospital.

Since most attacks against women are by men they know, you should practice self-defense techniques with partners you know, so that you can learn to defend yourself against people you know. When someone close to them tries to hurt them, women often think, "This can't be happening." A martial artist hesitates less. She knows a punch when she sees one, regardless of who is throwing it. She also knows how to block and counter it.

PRACTICING SELF-DEFENSE IN DAILY LIFE

Think of self-defense as something you do in your everyday life. There is no reason to live in fear, cowering behind a triple-locked door. Instead, assess possible threats as you go through your everyday life and make a plan for handling them. For instance, perhaps you wear a skirt and heels to work everyday. Experiment with performing your martial arts techniques in high heels. You will find that direct strikes (knee strikes, front kicks) work much better in this situation than kicks that require a pivot or a turn. Practice in your daily clothes to see what happens. And practice self-defense techniques in different areas. What happens when you try to perform a kick on a polished tile floor? Or in your backyard? Knowing these things ahead of time prevents nasty surprises later.

As you do your daily activities, be aware of your surroundings. Does your office become a desert after 5 p.m.? What would you do in the case of an attack? Do you know where doors, alarms, other people might be? Familiarize yourself with new locations. Where are stairwells, phones, escape routes?

Don't be afraid of seeming impolite. Step out of the elevator if you have a bad feeling about the person who just got on. Trust your instincts. Better to look a little foolish in the eyes of a complete stranger than to have the police fish your body out of the river because you didn't want to seem paranoid.

WHAT YOU SHOULD DEFEND

Because any self-defense situation has the potential to turn deadly, you should only fight when the alternative is serious physical harm. If someone grabs your purse, make a note of his physical characteristics and the getaway car he jumped into, and call the police. If someone walks into the restaurant where you wait tables and demands all the money in the cash register, give it to him. Heck, give him lunch to go while you're at it. These things aren't worth risking your physical well-being to prevent.

On the other hand, if you're physically threatened, take immediate, direct action. Not every woman is successful every time she resists an attack, but women who don't resist are never successful. Most women would rather fight and lose than succumb and have to live with their unwillingness to fight.

Although you should frequently practice the self-defense techniques described in the following chapters, be aware that any sort of resistance is better than none. If you can't quite remember how the defense against a wrist grab works, do the best you can with as much power and confidence as you can muster. The only caveat is this: if you intend to protect yourself, you must commit to your defense. Don't do a half-hearted block, or a faint, "no, please don't." Instead, hit as hard as you can, as often as you must; yell as loudly as you can, for as long as you have to. Don't irritate your attacker; stop him.

23

BASIC SELF-DEFENSE TECHNIQUES

Basic self-defense techniques have the primary purpose of allowing you to escape from a threatening situation. Of course, the simplest technique is sometimes the hardest: walking away. If you ever feel that a situation could quickly turn sour, or you don't like the direction a conversation is headed, you have the right to simply walk away and put some distance between you and the potential attacker.

Occasionally, you may not walk away in time. If the attacker kicks or punches, you can easily respond with one of the many Tae Kwon Do blocks and strikes you've learned. But often in a self-defense situation (particularly in the case of women), the attacker will grab you. The self-defense techniques described in this and the following chapters help you to respond to such a threat.

Tae Kwon Do teaches self-defense techniques to use in common scenarios. After practicing these pre-set responses, you'll respond quickly and appropriately to an attack. As you become more comfortable with the various self-defense techniques you learn, you can add your own ideas, tailoring your techniques to your own skills. When practicing, be sure the techniques described will work for you, and practice with partners both larger and smaller than you to get a feel for how your approach might need to vary.

Most of the drills described in this book ask you to begin in a fighting stance or other formal stance. When practicing self-defense techniques, however, you should approach the drills more naturally, as if you were going about your ordinary business.

AGAINST A WRIST GRAB

Escape Technique:

Work with a partner. The attacking partner grabs your opposite wrist with his hand. For instance, he grabs your right wrist with his left hand. Twist your hand away, pulling sharply (see figures 226 and 227). This technique is less effective when your partner grabs your same side wrist (i.e., he grabs your right wrist with his right hand). In this case, strike the attacker's forearm away using your free hand to perform a plam strike (see figures 231 and 232 for a similar technique).

| Figure 227 | Figure 228 |

AGAINST A TWO-WRIST GRAB

Escape Technique:

Work with a partner. The attacking partner grabs both of your wrists. Swing your arms upward, putting your hands into the knife hand position. Push down on your partner's wrists to force him to release you. Push your partner's hands away while stepping back (see figures 228, 229 and 230).

| Figure 228 | Figure 229 | Figure 230 |

AGAINST A SLEEVE GRAB

Escape Technique:

Working with a partner, facing each other, have your partner grab your sleeve or upper arm. With your free hand, perform a palm strike to your partner's arm to knock his grasp loose (see figures 231 and 232).

Figure 231   **Figure 232**

AGAINST A SHIRT/LAPEL GRAB

Escape Technique:

Working with a partner, facing each other, have your partner grab your shirt or jacket from the front. Reach over and peel your partner's hand away (see figures 233 and 234).

Figure 233   **Figure 234**

AGAINST A CHOKEHOLD

Escape Technique:

There are several variations for this.

1. When your partner performs the chokehold, push away his left arm by performing a palm strike to it with your right hand. Push away his right arm by performing a palm strike to it with your left hand. This releases your partner's grip so you can escape (see figures 235, 236 and 237).

| Figure 235 | Figure 236 | Figure 237 |

2. Working with your partner, facing each other, have your partner grab your throat with both hands. Slide both arms between his. Reach up over your head, turn quickly and escape (see figures 238 and 239).

| Figure 238 | Figure 239 |

AGAINST A TWO-WRIST GRAB FROM BEHIND

Escape Technique:

There are several variations for this.

1. Work with a partner. Have your partner grab both of your wrists from behind. Step to the side and twist sharply toward your partner. When you partner releases your hands, escape (see figures 240 and 241).

Figure 240

Figure 241

2. Step back toward your partner, lifting your farthest arm up high. Step through the opening and escape (see figures 242, 243 and 244).

Figure 242

Figure 243

Figure 244

AGAINST A SLEEVE GRAB FROM BEHIND

Escape Technique:

Work with a partner. Have your partner grab your sleeve from behind. Turn toward your partner, striking her arm with a palm strike. Knock your partner's arm away (see figures 245, 246 and 247).

| Figure 245 | Figure 246 | Figure 247 |

AGAINST A ONE-ARM CHOKEHOLD FROM BEHIND

Escape Technique:

There are several variations of this.

1. Work with a partner. Have your partner grab you in a one-arm chokehold from behind. Turn your head so that your throat rests in the crook of your partner's elbow. This ensures that you will be able to breathe even if your partner tightens the chokehold. Turn toward your partner and lean forward. Keep turning and pull your head free (see figures 248 and 249).

| Figure 248 | Figure 249 |

2. Have your partner perform a chokehold. Reach up, claw to his face and grab his arm. Turn toward your partner and lean down to loosen his grip. Push your partner backward to force him to release you (see figures 250, 251 and 252).

Figure 250   **Figure 251**

Figure 252

AGAINST A TWO-HANDED CHOKEHOLD FROM BEHIND

Escape Technique:

Work with a partner. Have your partner grasp your throat with both hands. Raise one arm, and turn toward your raised arm. Keep turning until you break your partner's grip (see figures 253 and 254 on the following page).

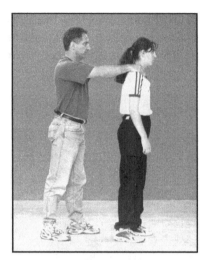 

Figure 253   **Figure 254**

24
INTERMEDIATE SELF-DEFENSE TECHNIQUES

The second level of self-defense is control. If the attacker persists or physically endangers you, your only choice is to convince him to stop. This may require more sophisticated self-defense techniques. The intermediate techniques that follow build on the basic techniques shown in the previous chapter. Continue to practice escape techniques, but also practice control techniques until you can do either without thinking.

JOINT LOCKS

Tae Kwon Do teaches the use of joint locks in self-defense. At the intermediate level, controling techniques rely on traps, holds and locks. Joint locks immobilize an opponent by manipulating his or her joints, usually by pushing or pulling the joint in the direction opposite to its natural movement. Locks can be applied to any joint and work as a method of controlling the opponent without causing permanent physical harm. You must use care when working with a partner, since you can dislocate a joint by applying too much pressure.

AGAINST A WRIST GRAB

Control Technique:

There are several variations.

1. Work with a partner. Face each other. Have your partner grab your wrist. Grip your partner's wrist with your free hand. Peel your partner's hand away, twisting his arm in an arc. Continue to twist your partner's hand to control it (see figures 255, 256 and 257 on the following page).

| Figure 255 | Figure 256 | Figure 257 |

2. When your partner grabs your wrist, grip his hand with your free hand. Turn your back toward your partner while stepping away. Pull your partner's arm over your shoulder with his palm facing up. When your partner's elbow rests on your shoulder, pull downward (see figures 258, 259, 260 and 261).

| Figure 258 | Figure 259 |

| Figure 260 | Figure 261 |

AGAINST A TWO-WRIST GRAB

Control Technique:

Working with a partner, both facing the same way, have your partner grab both of your wrists. Pull one hand free, as you would for a single wrist grab. With your free hand, trap your partner's other hand. Turn toward your partner and press the point of your elbow against your partner's elbow to create an arm lock (see figures 262, 263, 264 and 265).

Figure 262

Figure 263

Figure 264

Figure 265

Figure 266

Figure 267

Figure 268

Figure 269

AGAINST A SLEEVE GRAB

Control Technique:

Working with a partner, facing each other, have your partner grab your sleeve or upper arm. Raise your arm and wrap it around your partner's arm just above the elbow. Twist and lift to gain control of your partner (see figures 266, 267, 268 and 269).

Figure 270

Figure 271

Figure 272

Figure 273

AGAINST A SHIRT/LAPEL GRAB

Control Technique:

Working with a partner, facing each other, have your partner grab your shirt or jacket from the front. Grasp your partner's hand with your nearest hand, peeling your partner's hand away. With both hands, twist your partner's hand over so that his or her palm and elbow are facing upward. Continue twisting to keep control (see figures 270, 271, 272 and 273).

AGAINST A CHOKEHOLD

Control Technique:

When your partner performs the chokehold, hold one of his hands with one of yours. Turn toward your partner, trapping his or her arms between your arm and chest(see figures 274, 275 and 276).

Figure 274

Figure 275

Figure 276

AGAINST A TWO-WRIST GRAB FROM BEHIND

Control Technique:

Work with a partner. Have your partner grab both of your wrists from behind. Step to the side and raise your outside arm (and, therefore, your partner's arm.) Lower your body and slide under your partner's arm. Stand up. Twist your partner's arm behind his back to control it (see figures 277, 278 and 279).

Figure 277

Figure 278

Figure 279

AGAINST A SLEEVE GRAB FROM BEHIND

Control Technique:

Work with a partner. Have your partner grab your sleeve from behind. Turn toward your partner, making your hand a knife hand. Grab your partner's wrist. With your other hand, grab his shoulder. Twist your partner's wrist and press down on his shoulder. Continue pressing to control your partner (see figures 280, 281, 282 and 283).

Figure 280

Figure 281

Figure 282

Figure 283

AGAINST A ONE-ARM CHOKEHOLD FROM BEHIND

Control Technique:

Work with a partner. Have your partner grab you in a one-arm chokehold from behind. Turn so that your throat rests in the crook of your partner's elbow. This ensures that you will be able to breathe even if your partner tightens the chokehold. Grab your partner's arm at the wrist and elbow. Turn toward your partner and pull down on his arm. Pull free, holding onto your partner's wrist. Press your forearm to his elbow to control him (see figures 284, 285, 286 and 287).

Figure 284

Figure 285

Figure 286

Figure 287

AGAINST A TWO-HANDED CHOKEHOLD FROM BEHIND

Control Technique:

Work with a partner. Have your partner grasp your throat with both hands. Reach back and cover your partner's hands with your palms. Step away from partner, turn and lean forward. Continue gripping your partner's wrists to control his arms (see figures 288, 289 and 290).

Figure 288

Figure 289

Figure 290

25
ADVANCED SELF-DEFENSE TECHNIQUES

Advanced self-defense techniques should only be used when you know that you're in serious physical danger. Perhaps you've tried to escape or control the attacker and he still continues to attack, or maybe his initial attack is frightening enough that you know you must stop him immediately. In this case, you must remove the threat and launch a counterattack, thus allowing yourself to escape, injure your attacker enough to stop the attack or frighten your attacker so much that he stops the attack.

VITAL POINT STRIKES

At the advanced stage, you'll often attack the vital points of the body, which can be devastating to the attacker since these are the most vulnerable areas of the body. Vital point strikes are meant to cause physical harm to the opponent. Vital points vulnerable to strikes include the following:

Eye	Inner wrist
Temple	Solar plexus
Ear	Floating ribs
Nose	Small of back
Jaw	Kidney
Throat	Tailbone
Side of neck	Groin
Shoulder blade	Knee
Armpit	Achilles heel
Elbow	Instep

Vital point strikes can be used along with joint locks if the joint lock alone is not sufficient to stop the attacker. Remember these vulnerable areas as you practice self-defense techniques and develop your own tactics.

ARMED ATTACKERS

The techniques described in this self-defense section are for use against an unarmed attacker. Some of these techniques could be used against an armed attacker, but this requires special training. If someone intends to harm you and he is armed, you must decide to what extent you can and will fight unarmed. If the attacker seems certain to harm you regardless of whether you fight or not, then by all means you should fight. Think about self-defense scenarios ahead of time (although you never know how you will react when under pressure). By thinking ahead, if you ever find yourself facing an armed attacker, you will already have decided what route you want to take. If you believe that submitting will cause the least amount of harm to you, then, having decided that, accept it. But if you think an attacker is more likely to hurt you if you don't put up a fight, then be prepared to fight. Only you can decide which is the right course of action for you to take.

WEAPONS

People often purchase weapons, usually guns, for the purpose of protecting themselves, their loved ones and their property. All too often, guns and other weapons injure or kill innocent bystanders. If you choose to keep a weapon, you must be sure it is safe so that children (or others) do not accidentally hurt themselves or someone else. You must also ensure that your weapon is never used for anything but the most serious of self-defense situations. Unfortunately, weapons are often used to intimidate family members and friends during disagreements, with disastrous results. Finally, you must be willing to learn how to use the weapon, and you must be willing to use it. It is not as simple to aim a gun and shoot it as it might appear. Invest in lessons at a firing range. As with all skills, weapons use requires constant practice.

You must also ask yourself if you could really use a weapon against another person. You must imagine what this would feel like and then be convinced that you can do it. Otherwise, it is too easy for an attacker to use your own weapon against you. In general, weapons such as guns and knives are a danger to individuals and society at large, and conscientious martial artists should avoid them.

ENVIRONMENTAL WEAPONS

Ocasionally, it might be appropriate to use a weapon. But if you need additional help in fending off an attacker, your best bet is an environmental weapon. There are two reasons for this. First, an environmental weapon is unlikely to harm an innocent bystander. If you use it against an attacker, it is unlikely to actually kill him or her. Using excessive force even against a person with obvious criminal intentions can land you in jail. Second, environmental weapons are all around us and readily available, unlike other weapons. Unless your handgun is strapped to your thigh at all times, you can easily be caught unaware. The weapon you invested in will be useless if it's sitting in the dresser drawer and you're carjacked on the way home from work.

Environmental weapons include any object that can be used to strike, poke or distract an attacker. A telephone could add power to a strike; a pencil could be poked into an attacker's eye; a mug could be thrown.

Look around your home, school, office and other areas where you spend time. How many weapons do you see and how could you use them if you needed to? Don't forget that just as an attacker could use a gun or a knife, he could use an environmental weapon, too (see figures 291, 292, 293, 294, 295 and 296).

Figure 291

Figure 292

Figure 293

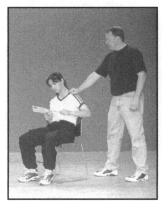

Figure 294

Figure 295

Figure 296

AGAINST A WRIST GRAB

Counterattack Technique:

There are several variations.

1. Work with a partner. Have your partner grab your right wrist with his right hand. Lean backward and deliver a right leg side kick to your partner's ribs (see figures 297 and 298).

Figure 297

Figure 298

2. When you partner grabs your right wrist, pull free and strike to the temple with a back fist (see figures 299, 300 and 301).

Figure 299

Figure 300

Figure 301

AGAINST A TWO-WRIST GRAB

Counterattack Technique:

Working with a partner, both facing each other, have your partner grab both of your wrists. Swing your arms up and twist your hands, pulling free. Perform a front kick to your partner's midsection or groin (see figures 302, 303 and 304).

Figure 302

Figure 303

Figure 304

AGAINST A SLEEVE GRAB

Counterattack Technique:

Working with a partner, facing each other, have your partner grab your sleeve or upper arm. Raise your arm and wrap it around your partner's arm just above the elbow. Then deliver a knee strike to your partner's midsection (see figures 305, 306 and 307).

Figure 305

Figure 306

Figure 307

AGAINST A SHIRT/LAPEL GRAB

Counterattack Technique:

Working with a partner, facing each other, have your partner grab your shirt or jacket from the front. Grasp your partner's hand with both of your hands. Twist your partner's hand over so that his or her palm and elbow face upward. Deliver a crescent kick to your partner's head (see figures 308, 309, 310 and 311).

Figure 308

Figure 309

Figure 310

Figure 311

AGAINST A CHOKEHOLD

Counterattack Technique:

When your partner performs the chokehold, strike to both sides of your partner's body with knife hands. This helps loosen your partner's hold. Then slide your arms up between his arms and spread your arms. As your partner releases his hold, strike to his or her neck with both hands. Then grab your partner's neck and pull him or her down. Drive a knee strike into your partner's chest (see figures 312, 313, 314, 315, 316 and 317).

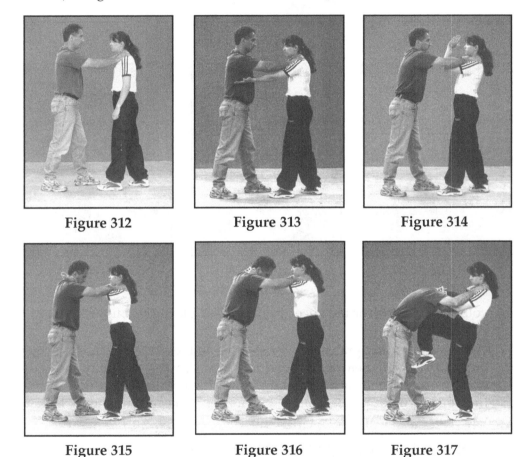

Figure 312   Figure 313   Figure 314

Figure 315   Figure 316   Figure 317

AGAINST A TWO-WRIST GRAB FROM BEHIND

Counterattack Technique:

There are several variations of this.
1. Work with a partner. Have your partner grab both of your wrists from behind. Step forward to move into kicking range. Kick straight back with

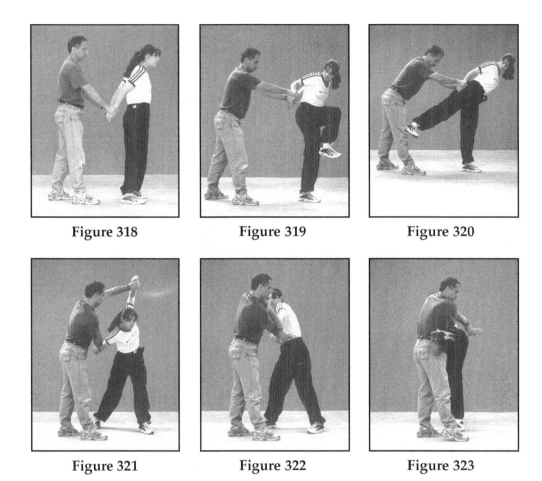

| Figure 318 | Figure 319 | Figure 320 |

| Figure 321 | Figure 322 | Figure 323 |

your heel, aiming for the knee, groin or solar plexus (see figures 318, 319 and 320).

2. When your partner grabs your wrists, step to the side while raising your outer arm (and, therefore, your partner's arm.) Lower your body and slide under your partner's arm. Stand up. Push down with your hands to control your partner's hands. Follow with a knee strike or roundhouse kick to your partner's solar plexus (see figures 321, 322 and 323).

AGAINST A SLEEVE GRAB FROM BEHIND

Counterattack Technique:

Work with a partner. Have your partner grab your sleeve from behind. Perform a backward elbow strike with your free arm, aiming for your partner's solar plexus. Then turn slightly and perform a backfist to your partner's face, (see figures 324, 325 and 326 on the following page).

| **Figure 324** | **Figure 325** | **Figure 326** |

AGAINST A ONE-ARM CHOKEHOLD FROM BEHIND

Counterattack Technique:

Work with a partner. Have your partner grab you in a one-arm chokehold from behind. Turn so that your throat rests in the crook of your partner's elbow. This ensures that you will be able to breathe even if your partner tightens the chokehold. Reach behind you and grab your partner's shirt, hair, or upper arm. Slide your foot behind his and pull down on his arm. Keep pulling and turn away to disrupt his balance. Throw your partner to the ground. Add a stomp to the ribs, if necessary (see figures 327, 328, 329 and 330).

| **Figure 327** | **Figure 328** | **Figure 329** |

Figure 330

Figure 331

Figure 332

Figure 333

Figure 334

AGAINST A TWO-HANDED CHOKEHOLD FROM BEHIND

Counterattack Technique:

Work with a partner. Have your partner grasp your throat with both hands. Raise one arm. Turn toward your raised arm. Keep turning until you break your partner's grip. Then follow with a palm strike to your partner's face (see figures 331, 332, 333 and 334).

SITUATIONAL SELF-DEFENSE

Consider how you can adapt these techniques (and others) to fit different circumstances. For example, if you were sitting when someone grabbed you

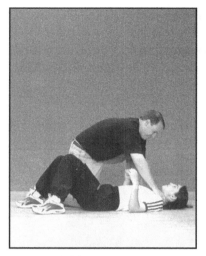

Figure 335

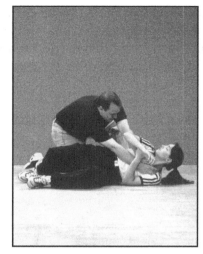

Figure 336

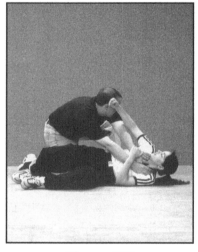

Figure 337

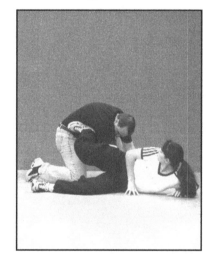

Figure 338

from behind, what would you do? Or, what if someone attacked while you were lying down (or if someone threw you to the ground)? Perhaps you could perform a modified hip throw while seated. How about scratching and biting? Use your fingernails, jewelry (a ring could scratch an attacker) and other personal objects (throw your purse or swing it at an attacker to distract him). Don't practice self-defense techniques only when you're in the middle of your martial arts workout (although that is also a good time to work on them). Practice and refine your techniques even when you aren't at class. If you think of a technique while at work, for example, practice it immediately. If this is not possible, write it down so that you can work on it at your next martial arts session (even bringing your office chair home with you if you have to). Always practice techniques several times in order to make sure it works the way you think it will. Occasionally, what seems like an excellent self-defense technique only works occasionally, or only works on a small portion of the people you try it with. The best self-defense techniques are simple, straightforward, easy to memorize, and can be used on almost anyone (see figures 335, 336, 337 and 338).

PART SEVEN:
MASTERING FORMS

26
FORMS PRACTICE

Forms (called "hyungs") are pre-set patterns of techniques and other movements that practitioners memorize. Depending on the style of Tae Kwon Do that you practice, you might learn a new form every month or two until you reach black belt level. Then you learn fewer forms but work on mastering all techniques. When you learn a form, you commit it to memory and continue to practice it so that you can perform the complete form without a mistake at any time. Therefore, you should continue to practice the form that you learn at the white belt level even when you're a black belt, so that you never forget it. Not only does this continually hone your skills, it helps you pass your skills on to other students.

WHY PRACTICE FORMS?

Forms are a convenient way to learn and then demonstrate martial arts techniques. Each form combines skill-level appropriate techniques together. At the white belt level, for example, the white belt form includes only a few techniques, ones that you learn within the first few weeks of training. As you progress through the ranks, the forms you memorize become more complex. Practicing forms allows you to practice new techniques, various stances, and the footwork needed to move from one position to another in the form.

You can practice a large number of techniques, footwork, and stances in a small amount of space because forms are designed so that you turn and move frequently, staying in a comparatively small area.

THE "ART" OF MARTIAL ARTS

In Tae Kwon Do, as in most other martial arts, forms practice and performance is the "art" in the system of fighting. Watching a form done well is something like watching an ice skater or ballroom dancer. The formal techniques used can be quite beautiful.

Because forms require endurance and power to perform well, they build strength and focus. Your goal is to practice your forms frequently enough so that your body, not just your mind, memorizes the routine and you do not have to think about it. This helps build confidence. Forms also give you an idea of how techniques can flow together, so that you can use parts of forms in step sparring or freestyle sparring.

HOW TO PRACTICE FORMS

Tae Kwon Do tournaments always have a forms division. Depending on the event, this might be an opportunity for you to show your creativity (creating your own form, setting your form to music, etc.) or it might be an opportunity for you to demonstrate your mastery of a particular traditional form.

When you practice forms, you must perfectly execute each technique. All chambers should be performed correctly; all strikes should land in the appropriate target area; all techniques should be performed smoothly and powerfully, without hesitation. In addition to perfect technique, you must use predetermined footwork to move to new positions. Practice this continually, making certain your feet move with precision and that you assume each new footwork pattern and each new stance perfectly. As you move from position to position, you must take care not to bounce. Often, as beginners move from one stance to another, they straighten their knees, rising up, then assume the new stance and bend their knees, lowering down. To a spectator, they look like they're bouncing up and down. To prevent "bounce," keep your knees bent between stances and as you move from position to position.

At the same time, you must breathe smoothly and evenly. Not only does this prevent you from turning blue and fainting, it helps keep fatigue from setting in before the end of the form, and it indicates your control.

Some practitioners think that forms are easy compared to other parts of marital arts training. These people aren't performing their forms correctly. Even though a form might contain fewer than 20 techniques, you should be sweating and breathing hard when you're finished. You must execute each technique as if you were striking an attacker. You must perform each technique perfectly, so that if the form calls for a high kick, you don't cheat and perform a middle kick when you're tired. The practice of forms is an area where the tenet of integrity comes in. Only you know and can tell how much energy and effort you put into your forms practice, and you owe it to yourself and to Tae Kwon Do to practice forms tirelessly, continuously and powerfully.

27
CHON-JI FORM

Traditional Tae Kwon Do forms have a symbolic aspect and are named after important people or concepts in Korean history. The shape of a pattern may refer to an ideogram — that is, a written character that stands for a Korean word. The number of movements in a form may have special significance. All of this helps practitioners understand something about the Korean culture. A truly respectful practitioner of Tae Kwon Do will research and investigate details about Korean culture in order to understand and appreciate the art of Tae Kwon Do.

THE MEANING OF CHON-JI HYUNG

Chon-ji (pronounced "chun-gee") form is the first form a Tae Kwon Do student learns. Chon-ji means heaven and earth and refers to the beginning of both the world and of human history. Since it evokes beginnings, it is the beginner form. There are two parts to the pattern: the first part represents heaven and the second part represents earth. A total of 19 techniques make up the form. Each technique should be performed with equal power, balance, agility and grace.

CHON-JI HYUNG

The pattern of the Chon-Ji form is in the shape of a cross. To perform it, you must assume that four opponents are challenging you, one from the front, one from the back and one from each side. The techniques used are ready stance, low block (in a front stance), straight punch (in a front stance) and inside-outside crescent block (in a back stance).

Figure 339

Figure 340

In all forms, you should keep your eyes forward, with no looking around. The only time you should deviate from this is when you are specifically instructed to look in a certain direction. Otherwise, keep your eyes up and focus on what is directly ahead of you.

BEGIN PART I

Begin in the ready stance. Look to the left to see your first attacker (see figures 339 and 340).

MOVEMENT 1

Step and turn to the left with your left leg, moving into a front stance with your left leg forward. As you move, low block with your left arm over your left leg. You should be at a 90-degree angle to your starting position (see figure 341).

Figure 341

MOVEMENT 2

Step forward with your right leg, moving into a front stance. At the same time, perform a straight punch to the middle section with your right hand. Keep your arm extended (see figure 342 on the following page).

MOVEMENT 3

Turn and step 180 degrees to your right, moving into a front stance with your right leg forward. As you move, perform a low block with your right arm over your right leg (see figure 343 on the following page).

Figure 342

Figure 343

Figure 344

Figure 345

MOVEMENT 4

Step forward with your left leg, moving into a front stance. At the same time, perform a straight punch to the middle section with your left hand. Stand in a strong front stance, your arm extended (see figure 344).

MOVEMENT 5

Pick up your left leg and turn 90 degrees. Assume a strong front stance, facing the same direction as when you started. As you move into position, perform a low block with your left arm over your left leg (see figure 345).

Figure 346

Figure 347

MOVEMENT 6

Step forward with your right leg, moving into a front stance. As you move, perform a straight punch to the middle section with your right hand. Stay in a strong front stance, your arm extended, your eyes forward (see figure 346).

MOVEMENT 7

Turn and step 180 degrees to the right, moving into a strong front stance, your right leg forward. As you move into position, perform a low block with your right arm over your right leg (see figure 347).

MOVEMENT 8

Step forward with your left leg, moving into a front stance. As you move, perform a straight punch to the middle section with your left hand. Stay in a strong front stance, your arm extended, your eyes forward (see figure 348).

END OF PART I

You have finished the first part of the pattern. You may wish to repeat it several times before going on to the second part, as it is often easier to memorize new skills by breaking them into smaller pieces.

Figure 348

BEGIN PART II

The second part of the pattern begins here. You should be/remain in the same position as at the end of Part I.

MOVEMENT 9

Step and turn with your left leg, moving 90 degrees from your starting position. Assume a strong back stance, with most of the weight on your back leg (your right leg). As you turn, perform an inside-outside crescent block with your left arm. Make sure you perform a strong block above your left leg (see figure 349).

Figure 349

Figure 350

Figure 351

MOVEMENT 10

Stepping forward with your right leg, perform a straight punch with your right hand to the middle section. You should be in a strong front stance, your arm extended, your eyes forward (see figure 350).

MOVEMENT 11

Turn and step right 180 degrees, performing an inside-outside block with your right arm as you turn. Move into a strong back stance (see figure 351).

Figure 352

Figure 353

MOVEMENT 12

Step forward with your left leg, moving into a front stance, and perform a straight punch with your left hand to the middle section. You should be in a strong front stance, your arm extended, eyes forward (see figure 352).

MOVEMENT 13

Turn and step left 90 degrees, performing an inside-outside block with your left arm as you turn. Step into a back stance, making sure your position is solid and strong (see figure 353).

MOVEMENT 14

Step forward with your right leg, moving into a front stance, and perform a straight punch with your right hand to the middle section. You should be in a strong front stance, your arm extended, eyes forward (see figure 354).

MOVEMENT 15

Turn and step right 180 degrees, until you are facing the position in which you started the form. Move into a back stance, performing an inside-outside block as you move into position (see figure 355 on the following page).

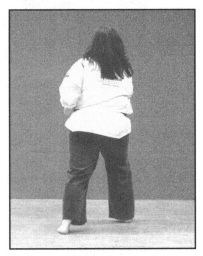

Figure 354

Figure 355

Figure 356

Figure 357

Figure 358

MOVEMENT 16

Step forward with your left leg, moving into a front stance, and perform a straight punch with your left hand to the middle section. You should be in a strong front stance, your arm extended, eyes forward (see figure 356).

MOVEMENT 17

Take another step forward, this time with your right leg, punching with your right hand to the middle section as you go. You should end in a strong front stance (see figure 357).

Figure 359

Figure 360

MOVEMENT 18

Next, step back with your right leg, punching with your left hand to the middle section as you go. You should end in strong front stance with your left leg forward and your left hand extended (see figure 358 on the previous page).

MOVEMENT 19

Finally, step back with your left leg, punching with your right hand to the middle section as you go. You should end in a strong front stance with your right leg forward and your right hand extended. Kihop loudly as you finish the form (see figure 359).

END OF THE FORM

After you have finished the form, return to the ready position (see figure 360).

PART EIGHT:
PRACTICAL ADVICE

28
AVOIDING INJURY

Although practicing the martial arts can lead to injury, it isn't inevitable. Taking sensible precautions can prevent some of the most common injuries. For instance, warming up and stretching before a vigorous workout and cooling down afterward can prevent common strains and sprains.

Because women are more prone to certain injuries than men, they should pay particular attention to preventing these injuries. Women have hip and knee injuries more frequently than men, while men have more trouble with hamstring and groin pulls. Overall, the most common injuries in martial arts practice are overuse injuries, hyperextension injuries, and sprains and strains.

It should go without saying that you should always seek medical advice for any injury or unexplained swelling, tenderness or pain.

OVERUSE INJURIES

Overuse injuries occur when a joint is used repetitively, especially when the joint is not accustomed to the use.

1.) *Tendinitis and bursitis.* The two most common overuse injuries can cause pain and discomfort in a joint when an individual begins using the joint more than usual. To prevent this problem, stretch before working out and execute techniques precisely. On a turning kick, if you don't pivot correctly, you'll put undue stress on your hips and knees, which can cause overuse injuries and other damage.

Although painful and frustrating, overuse injuries rarely cause more than temporary discomfort. If you suspect you have an overuse injury, check with your physician. Visiting with a sports medicine specialist or even a sports trainer can help you to learn how to prevent such problems.

Usually rest, ice, and an anti-inflammatory such as ibuprofen (or in more extreme cases, a prescription medication) will ease the problem. If not, your doctor may recommend an injection of cortisone and/or physical therapy treatment.

While overuse injuries can affect all joints, for women hips and knees are most commonly overused, followed by the shoulders. Most women don't have the same amount of upper body strength as their male counterparts. Since martial arts utilize a variety of hand, elbow and arm techniques, your shoulders undergo more stress and strain than usual. Since the muscle mass is usually not as well-developed here as in other parts of the body, these stresses and strains are more likely to cause an injury. Remember to stretch all of your joints before you start training and to perform techniques exactly as described. Add weight training for strength.

2.) *Stress Fractures.* Stress fractures usually occur over a period of time. A bone that must withstand repeated blows may develop a break or a series of small fissures that have the effect of a fracture. In martial arts these kinds of fractures occasionally occur, usually in a foot or hand. Using proper technique and limiting the amount of abuse you direct toward any one area of your body can help prevent such an injury. A stress fracture can feel similar to a broken bone, or it can feel like an overuse injury.

HYPEREXTENSION INJURIES

Hyperextension occurs when a joint moves beyond its usual stopping point. This can happen when you throw a punch or kick with full energy but no target absorbs the energy of the strike. Kicking the heavy bag will rarely cause a hyperextension injury because the heavy bag absorbs the energy and power of the kick. But when you kick air (as you do when practicing in training class or in front of a mirror), your energy isn't absorbed and your momentum isn't stopped. Therefore, your arm or leg can move beyond its normal range and hyperextend a joint.

To prevent hyperextension, always keep your joints slightly bent. Never fully extend and lock out a knee or elbow joint.

You can easily identify hyperextension. Sudden pain in a joint after you execute a technique or pain that persists whenever you use the affected limb, indicates a possible hyperextension. Rest, ice, anti-inflammatories and, if pain continues or worsens, a visit to the doctor are all called for.

ACUTE INJURIES

Strains, sprains, tears, cuts and bruises result from an acute injury — that is, a single event that happens suddenly and causes an injury. Perhaps you roll your wrist when your punch lands, and you end up with a sprain. Sprains and strains can range from mild to severe. The milder cases require little attention, perhaps some aspirin and some ice. More serious cases require rest, ice, compression and elevation, a treatment also known by its acronym "RICE."

1.) *Strain.* The usual signs of a strain include pain, tenderness and swelling. If the muscle doesn't seem to work at all, seek treatment immediately. Surgery may be necessary to repair the damage.

A muscle strain happens when you overstretch a muscle. The word "pull" is often used to describe a strain. The muscle continues to function — it just becomes sore. More serious strains may result in muscle tears, which require more time and rest to heal. In martial arts, the most common strains occur in the hamstring and the groin area. For women, the hip flexors (the small muscles running from the hip to the top of the thigh) are commonly affected.

Most strains are quick to mend. Put ice on the area intermittently for 24 hours. After a day, you can use a heating pad. A few days of rest is usually sufficient for healing.

To prevent strains, warm up and stretch before working out. Also, if you are prone to strains, incorporate weight training and other conditioning exercises into your fitness program.

2.) *Sprain.* A sprain occurs when the ligaments that connect muscles to bones are injured. Usually a twist, a misstep or an extreme stretch puts too much strain on the ligaments, and tissue is torn. Sprains commonly happen to the ankles and knees. Signs include rapid swelling, reduced ability to use the affected area and pain. If you actually hear a snapping sound, seek treatment immediately. You may have a detached ligament. Surgery is sometimes needed to repair the damage.

For routine sprains, ice, compression and rest will cure the condition. The sprained part can usually bear weight after a day or two, but remember this doesn't mean it is completely healed. For a few weeks, minimize your workout intensity to avoid worsening the sprain. If the sprain is severe or the joint is unstable, the area may need to be immobilized with a cast or splint. If you repeatedly strain or sprain a certain part of your body, use a brace, wrap or tape to help support the area and prevent progressive damage to the area. Consult your physician, who can recommend a sports trainer or a physical therapist for tips on preventing recurring injuries.

3.) *Cuts and Bruises.* Bruises and cuts are probably the most common martial arts-related injuries. Usually, some ice or a bandage will suffice. For more serious cases, you may need to visit the doctor. Bleeding that won't stop is a sign to seek medical help.

Rest, ice, compression, and elevation can help bruises heal. See a doctor if the injury doesn't improve or if there's the possibility of a fracture. Use pads when sparring to lessen bruising and cuts. When practicing take down moves, practice on mats that cushion the fall.

4.) *Fractures.* Fractures aren't always obvious. Pain, loss of function, and swelling indicate the possibility of a fracture, but the symptoms sometimes resemble the symptoms of a sprain. X-rays may be needed to determine the extent of an injury. Some fractures, such as with the small bones of the feet or hands, cannot be treated very well, except by resting the affected area. Sometimes you can tape the injured finger or toe to the one next to it to provide additional support and prevent further trauma.

Fractures heal slowly, over weeks or even months. Usually, the broken bone must be kept immobile through the use of a cast or splint. Sometimes screws or a plate must be attached to help the bone heal. Traction and bed rest are necessary only when a broken bone is difficult to keep immobile, such as a pelvic bone. A fractured bone may require physical therapy treatment. Otherwise, muscle tone is lost, stiffness occurs and healing is slower.

5.) *Dislocations.* Dislocations usually happen after an acute injury. A dislocation occurs when the ends of the bones of the joint slip out of their normal place and position, causing pain, swelling and difficulty using the affected joint. Sometimes a dislocation will injure nearby muscles and ligaments. Seek treatment immediately to distinguish a dislocation from a fracture, to determine the extent of damage and to prevent further damage to the surrounding tissues. Usually the dislocation is easily corrected and the area is immobilized for a few days.

Do not resume full-speed training until your physician has cleared it. You can re-injure the joint and even cause permanent damage and disability. Physical therapy may also help strengthen the surrounding muscles and ligaments to prevent a recurrence of a dislocation.

6.) *Back Injuries.* Injuries and strains to the back should always be treated with care because of the possible involvement of the spinal column. Spinal cord injuries are rare, but the possibility exists. Any sharp pain in the back should be treated. Unexplained tenderness or swelling may be signs of concern and should be checked out as well.

A note of caution: If you're taking painkillers or other medications (over the counter or prescription), make sure you know how your body handles them before you start working out. Some medications cause nausea and vomiting (not ideal when you're working out vigorously); others cause dizziness, which could interfere with your balance (not a good problem for a martial artist to have) and still others make you tired and sluggish (not the best condition to spar in). Further, painkillers can mask your body's signals, and you might re-injure yourself or cause a new injury if you are not careful. Ask your doctor or pharmacist about possible side effects.

Although it is not uncommon to have martial arts-related injuries, they can often be prevented if you use your common sense. Any fitness program should include a warm-up, stretching, the exercise itself, and a cool down. In many martial arts schools, you'll be responsible for your own warming up, stretching and cooling down. Don't try to save time by skipping these essential steps. Instead, make them part of your workout and help prevent injuries.

29
PARTICIPATING IN COMPETITION

Some women thrive on competition. Others avoid competition whenever possible. But all martial artists should take advantage of the opportunity to compete, at least occasionally.

Countless of these opportunities exist in the martial arts, including informal competitions encountered in daily practice. Sometimes you even compete against yourself to improve your techniques or better your speed.

Sometimes you can compete in friendly matches during class or more formally during practice by having "judges" — other students or instructors — look over your practice and evaluate you. But formal competition in the martial arts — the martial arts tournament — is a challenging, exhilarating and rewarding activity whether you win or lose.

STRETCHING YOUR LIMITS

Martial artists often question themselves. They ask, "Could I really defend myself?" and "Am I really strong enough or skillful enough to prevent a personal attack?" Performing in competition can help you gain more confidence and can help you believe that the answer is yes. It doesn't matter whether you score a lot of points, win first place or don't place at all. What matters is confronting your fear and overcoming it.

This takes practice. Participating in tournaments gives you confidence. Repeated practice increases your confidence. The first competition may make you so nervous that you fail. And that's OK. The next time, you'll be more comfortable because you'll know what to expect.

Competing shouldn't be the only way you measure yourself. It's just one yardstick. Some excellent martial artists don't compete for philosophical reasons. Others don't do well in competition but make excellent teachers or role models. Sometimes competitions don't showcase our true talents. We each find our own niche in martial arts. So when you go to compete, go to enjoy the experience and don't make too much from winning or losing.

Participating in a safe, well-run tournament is, of course, not the same as being confronted by a knife-wielding, drugged-out attacker in a dark alley, but that is not the point. Competition organizers will restrict the techniques you can use by making knee and elbow strikes illegal and putting any target area below the belt off-limits. In a real confrontation, any technique can be used, and any part of the body can be attacked. But truly dangerous techniques have no place in a tournament. Instead, they should be practiced under controlled conditions with familiar partners. Nonetheless, withstanding the pressure of tournament competition is an excellent experience. Even if you have never competed before in a physical contest and see no reason to start now, you'll find tournament competition (at least now and then) well worth the investment of time and energy.

OBTAINING COMPETITION INFORMATION

Since lack of experience or preparation can lead to frustrating and disappointing experiences, obtain as much information as possible about the tournament before you participate. Higher-ranking students, who usually have more competition experience than lower-ranking belts, make good sources of information.

If your school is invited to a competition, your head instructor will receive competition information that describes the rules of the tournament. For open tournaments (no invitation needed), find out more by reading martial arts magazines and visiting martial arts websites.

If you have an instructor, don't participate in a tournament without her permission. When you compete at a tournament, you represent your school, and it is up to your instructor to decide what tournaments are appropriate for her students to enter.

TOURNAMENT BASICS

Most Tae Kwon Do instructors actively encourage and sponsor martial arts competitions. These range from small in-school tournaments designed to give students a sense of what a tournament is about, to local competitions attended by students from a handful of nearby schools, to regional tournaments drawing from several states, to national and international competitions. It makes sense to start small to reduce the amount of anxiety you may have. Before participating in a big tournament, you may want to attend one as a spectator to see what is expected of competitors.

Many kinds of tournaments exist. Invitational tournaments require a specific invitation by the sponsoring organization. Open tournaments can be entered by anyone with a clean uniform. Smaller invitationals usually consist of one martial art style — Tae Kwon Do only, for instance. Larger tournaments may have multiple styles participating.

Divisions are much more specific at these large, multi-style tournaments than at one-style-only tournaments. The division is the group of people you will specifically compete against, since, of course, it would be unfair for 7-year old kids to compete against adult men. In small, one-style tournaments, the divisions are simple and straightfoward. Each event is divided into adult's and children's divisions. Children's divisions, generally co-ed, are usually grouped according to age. Older teenagers may be divided into divisions based on gender. The adult groups are divided into men's and women's divisions. There is often an executive division for older participants. Some tournaments have instructor's divisions so that instructors can compete without competing against their own students.

The groups are further divided by belt level, so that beginning, intermediate, and advanced practitioners compete against people of roughly the same skill level. In bigger tournaments, groups will be further divided by light, middle and heavy weight, which may be determined by height rather than weight, depending on the conference organizers. At local and regional tournaments, a division will be something like "Black Belt Women's Sparring," which makes it simple. If you're a black belt woman competing in sparring, this is your division.

In bigger competitions, organizers use additional criteria to create divisions, such as hard or soft style, weapons or empty-hand, and so on. This is more confusing, but it gives you more options and you're more likely to compete against people who are roughly similar to you in size, age, weight and skill level.

THE EVENTS

Tae Kwon Do tournaments have three basic contests: forms, sparring and breaking. In forms competition, you're judged on the performance of your form. You should select a form that best displays your talents and is appropriate to your skill level. Judges evaluate you on control, power and technique. In a contest including multiple styles, forms competition will be broken into soft styles, such as Wushu (Kung Fu) and hard styles, such as Tae Kwon Do. These groups may be further divided into weapons and empty hand forms. Some tournaments offer musical forms competition. Here judges evaluate artistic flair and harmony with the music. Some tournaments include pair or group forms, and in this case, judges also assess the synchronicity of the participants.

In most cases, a panel of five judges score the form from one to 10. Sometimes the highest and lowest scores will be disregarded. Rarely does one who completes a form achieve less than a five.

In breaking contests, usually limited to Tae Kwon Do competitions and a few Karate tournaments, you attempt to break a specified number of boards with techniques appropriate to your skill level. The number of boards varies by belt rank, with black belts breaking more boards than white belts. You're judged on the difficulty of your techniques, the correctness of your techniques, your ability to move quickly and smoothly from one technique to the next, and whether you break your boards on the first try. Again, five judges score the attempt from one to 10. The competitor with the highest score wins. If two competitors tie, the judges will select the technique for the tie-breaker.

Figure 361

In board breaking competition, the most important rule is to break the boards on the first try. Use techniques you're confident of, be sure the board holders are holding correctly for your techniques, and strike with confidence (see figure 361).

In Tae Kwon Do sparring, matches take place in two (sometimes three) minute rounds. In competition, you can expect contact. Participants may be required to wear protective gear. For a technique to score, it must be correctly performed and it must be unblocked. In some tournaments, the strike must cause a visible shock to the body of the opponent. Usually, hand techniques to the head aren't allowed, although kicks to the head are acceptable.

A center ring judge who acts as a referee and four corner judges determine the scoring in a match. A majority of judges must see the point and agree that it counts. In some competitions, a panel of judges (five plus the center ring judge) will score the match independently and the winner will be determined by decision. Fouls are called for stepping out of bounds on purpose, for using throws or takedowns, for avoiding the fight and other infringements. These result in the penalty of a point deduction. Foot techniques earn higher scores than hand techniques; jumping techniques score higher than standing techniques; a kick to the face is worth more than one to the body. When preparing for sparring in tournament, remember these guidelines and practice according to them. This will help you gain the most points possible in competition.

Tournament sparring usually calls for a break when a point has been called. The center ring judge, hearing a corner judge yell "point!" separates the contestants, stops the sparring, and then asks how many corner judges saw a point. If a majority did, then a point will be awarded. The official scorekeeper waits for the specific directive of the center ring judge before recording a point.

Usually time keeps running while points are decided, but sometimes it does not. This is important to know, because a two-minute bout in which time keeps running allows far fewer scoring opportunities than the bout in which time is stopped whenever tournament action stops.

Since practice sparring is usually continuous, the way action stops during a tournament match can interfere with your strategy, especially if you use a countering style of sparring. In this case, the opponent may land the first blow, which you would usually counter. But if the action stops while the judges decide if that first blow counted for a point, that countering technique you planned won't get you anywhere. It doesn't matter what the judge's decision is — point or not, you go back to your starting position and begin again.

You might work with a partner and just informally pause and step back to acknowledge when your partner has landed a technique that might be considered a point. If your partner will do the same whenever you execute a technique that might be called a point, both of you will improve your tournament sparring skills.

In this type of competition, you always know how many points you and your opponent have. This can be frustrating when your opponent is several points ahead of you. If you're several points ahead of her, it may cause you to lay back or enter a prevent defense, which may win football games but does not win sparring matches. If you practice sparring for points, you'll learn to anticipate and overcome your reactions and tendencies before you enter the tournament ring.

Sometimes sparring matches are continuous, however, with the judges scoring independently. This is an equally difficult type of match to fight, but for different reasons. First of all, you never know the score, so you have no idea of how aggressive you need to be. You have no idea what types of techniques the judges are seeing and counting, so you can't rearrange your strategy to account for that. It is difficult enough to spar when you know how you are doing, but it is much more difficult — and disconcerting — when you have no idea how the judges think you're doing.

The best way to spar a continuous, independently judged matched is to yell loud, and stick your kicks and punches and block aggressively so that no one will think that front kick snuck through your guard.

PREPARING FOR COMPETITION

Specific rules for tournaments will vary according to the organizers. Know the rules before you enter. Be aware, however, that tournaments are fluid events. It pays to be flexible. Perhaps you're an older woman who plans to enter the executive division, which the rules state is for people 35 and over. Sometimes, especially in women's competition at the local and regional level, only a few women will register for the executive division, so the division will be cancelled, and you'll be expected to join the regular women's division, where you'll get to compete against college kids who have never pulled a hamstring. Don't be surprised if, one day, as a brown belt, you find yourself in a division with yellow belts (slightly more advanced than white belts). This can seem unfair to both you and the yellow belt, but those who accept such changes and rethink their strategy to meet the new circumstances, are more likely to win.

To prepare for competition, practice according to the published rules of the tournament, but prepare for otherwise unexpected changes in those rules. By practicing according to the tournament rules, you'll be much more comfortable and confident come competition time.

As you prepare for competition, encourage your martial arts partners to imitate the tournament atmosphere. If you stay after class to practice your form, ask a higher ranking student to judge your performance. As you practice sparring, ask the instructor if she would call out points as she sees them, or have a group of tournament-goers set up a ring, with everyone taking turns practicing and judging. This helps you understand that sometimes you'll score a point but the judges won't see it, or not enough judges will see it. You need a majority, and if you let that frustrate you, you won't be able to win. You'll be flustered, angry or resentful, none of which will keep your attention focused where it should be.

Talk to veterans tournament-goers, including people who have been to the specific tournament you're planning to participate in and those who just have lots of tournament experience in general. They can help you understand what the judges are looking for.

Know the rules, consult with others who have been there and done that, and remember that even if you don't take away a trophy, you'll take away some excellent lessons.

30
PRACTICAL MATTERS

Women who have been active most of their lives have developed methods for handling practical concerns. For those not in that category, advice from the experienced can help.

MENSTRUATION AND STRESS INCONTINENCE

For those of us who menstruate or have stress incontinence (perhaps from child-bearing), simple problems occur. With all that kicking and stretching, it is easy to leak. Sometimes women avoid training during their period because of this concern, but that's not a good solution at all. First, remind yourself that no one cares. Adults should be able to handle it, kids ignore it, only you are worried about it.

Some women will use two forms of protection to help prevent leaks. Some wear disposable absorbent undergarments. These work well for women whose menstrual periods are heavy. Disposable undergarments are, indeed, cumbersome, and may restrict movement slightly. If you feel self-conscious, get the next size larger uniform so it fits more loosely. Biker shorts, made from stretchable, form-fitting material, can be worn under your workout clothes. You can find biker shorts in the women's athletic wear department of most bigger clothing stores.

Since the menstrual cycle occasionally causes bloating and tenderness, you may want to keep a looser fitting practice outfit around for those days. You may feel tired, sluggish and weak. While this can't be overcome, instead of becoming frustrated, redirect your martial arts goals. Work on stretching more during those times when you feel as if your speed is lacking. Practice forms if you can't bear the thought of bag kicking.

If necessary, take pain relievers to help with cramps, and drink plenty of water before class. You'll probably become fatigued more quickly and easily because you have less iron in your blood than usual. Your doctor can advise you on using supplemental iron tablets.

MENOPAUSE

In menopause, your hormone levels vary, so your energy level varies. You may be more sensitive to climate and suffer hot flashes and experience headaches. Exercise can help ease these conditions. It also helps maintain strong bones and muscles.

You may be more prone to injury during and after menopause than you were before. Thus, it is especially important to take steps to prevent injury. In addition, good stretching can help you maintain flexibility, which many women complain is their first physical ability to go. Continuing martial arts training — even starting martial arts training — will keep you strong and flexible physically and mentally throughout the rest of your life.

PREGNANCY

Female martial artists often wonder what happens when they become pregnant. What will they do now? The good news is that pregnant women who exercised regularly before pregnancy can continue to do so during and after pregnancy, though you must remember to keep your workouts reasonable. Exercise can help you have an easier labor, faster recovery, and more stamina after delivery.

Pregnancy is *not* the time start a martial arts class or an intense fitness program. Even if you've been working out regularly, check with your doctor before continuing to work out.

As your pregnancy progresses, you'll have to modify what you can do. Don't get discouraged by this. Above all, don't quit! Just slow down a bit. Remember that because of changes in your body, you're more easily injured during pregnancy than at any other time. Your weight distribution and center of gravity shift, making you more likely to lose your balance and fall.

Avoid exercises that require you to lay on your back. This could restrict blood flow to the fetus. You may become tired faster than usual, and you should listen to your body. Now is not the time to push it. Drink plenty of fluids and avoid working out when it's extremely hot and humid.

Stop sparring as soon as you find out you're pregnant. You should also perform other techniques with no contact in order to prevent accidental blows to your abdomen. Although your body will protect your baby quite well, it makes sense not to take unnecessary risks.

Modify your martial arts practice as needed. For instance, even if you have to avoid jumping kicks, you can still focus on the fundamentals — front kicks, side kicks, roundhouse kicks — which will help you remain sharp and focused.

Listen to your body, don't push, and you can continue working toward your martial arts goals even when you're nine months along.

AFTER CHILDBIRTH

Your recovery period after childbirth may be only a few weeks, but in the case of a very difficult delivery or a C-section, it may be six or eight weeks before your doctor clears you to return to working out. During this period, think about your martial arts practice even though you can't work out. As your doctor allows you, add in some light exercise, such as stretching. You can stretch while your baby naps. Walk instead of parking the car near the front door of the grocery store. Do more lifting and carrying as you get closer to full strength.

Read up on Tae Kwon Do as you recover. Learn about different kinds of martial arts — you may be able to use something that you learn. Watch videos during those times when you'd normally work out. Examine what they do, how they do it, and why they do it.

As you ease your way back to a full workout, don't worry if you're not up to full speed right away. Take your time, go slow, and you'll get back on track.

PREPARING FOR THE WORKOUT

Don't eat just before you work out. The digestive process will make you sluggish. But an empty stomach won't fuel your workout, so eat a small snack, nothing more substantial than an apple, about an hour before you plan to work out. Drink several glasses of water to fill up on fluids during the hour before your workout. Try a sports drink with extra carbohydrates in addition to water. Stop the liquids about 20 minutes before class. Drinking at least 16 ounces and preferably 24 ounces of water before working out will keep your stomach full, without diverting energy to digestion. A sports drink will give your body carbohydrates to fuel your workout, as will an apple or other small snack. This will help you to feel less tired and more energetic.

DRESSING FOR CLASS

One of the first things you'll discover is that everything from practice uniforms to headgear is made to fit men. This doesn't mean that there aren't good pieces of equipment for women — just that they aren't obvious. It requires some patience to find the things you need.

Unless otherwise specified, all equipment and uniforms are in men's sizes. This means that for women, regardless of the size they order, the uniform will fit strangely. All pants are cut with waist and hips of relatively similar proportion. Thus, if you get pants to fit your hips, the waist will be huge. If you get pants that fit your waist, they will pull up no further than the middle of your thighs. Tops don't have darts. If your chest size is medium or larger, a uniform that fits across your bust line will be too long and the sleeves will hang past your fingertips. For these problems, a seamstress can help. If you're handy with a needle, you can handle the simple revisions that make the uniform more comfortable.

All uniforms should fit loosely, allowing for comfortable movement in all ranges. But you shouldn't have to worry about your pants sliding down, or your top gaping open. Simple darts in the top will improve the fit. For sleeves that are too long, simply roll them up and stitch a few stitches to keep them in place. Or, hem the sleeves. Additional snaps or velcro closures on tops will help them stay securely closed. Many women wear T-shirts beneath the uniform top to prevent overexposure.

For pants, darts at the back can improve fit. Also, many women prefer elastic waistbands to the drawstring type. If the elasticized pants have a waist that is too big, replace the elastic with a smaller length of a tighter weave. Hem up pants that are too long. Some women like to buy a few uniforms at a time and fix them all at once.

Don't wear makeup. It runs, smears on the uniform, and gets in your eyes. Trim your nails — fingernails and toenails both. Artificial nails of any kind can be dangerous, especially if they catch on loose clothing. Also, long fingernails can be dangerous to your partners.

If your hair gets in the way as you practice, consider a shorter cut or keep it pulled back. If you don't want to pull it back in a pony tail because that causes breakage, consider a loose braid. This keeps hair out of your face, and since it is loosely braided, causes less damage to your hair. To keep sweat out of your eyes — and if you have lots of hair, your scalp will sweat more — tie a rolled-up bandanna around your forehead. This absorbs perspiration, looks OK (martial artists can wear headbands if they want) and also helps to keep your hair out of your eyes.

PURCHASING UNIFORMS

Most karate-type uniforms are sold in a strange set of sizes: 000 to 7 — 000 is for the smallest children, and seven is for the biggest men (both height and weight are taken into account when measuring for martial arts uniforms). Women who wear petite sizes, and who are size eight and under will fit into a size three; women up to about 5'6" and 170 can wear a four; taller and heavier women will find a five a better choice.

For sparring equipment, keep in mind that men's sizes are about one size larger than women's. Small gloves will fit a woman with medium-sized hands. For footgear, usually sold in small, medium and large sizes, it's helpful to know that a small fits a woman's foot size six to seven. Medium fits eight and nine. Large fits size ten and above. If you wear a smaller size than a six, and an extra small is not available, try children's shoe sizes.

Martial arts shoes and sometimes footgear are often sold in regular men's sizes. Men's 3 – 13 is the usual range. Men's shoes are about a size and a half larger than women's. A woman who wears a size 9 shoe will probably be comfortable in a men's size seven-and-a-half or eight. Again, foot width as well as length and personal comfort will affect the actual size that works best, but these measurements should give you an idea of where to begin.

ROLE MODEL

One of the consequences of the gender-related stereotypes we all suffer from is that you'll be the standard by which other women are judged—which can be a bit of a burden, if you think about it. As a female martial artist, it's important to be a good role model for other women and girls, too.

For this reason, you'll have to develop even more perseverance and self-control than male martial artists do. But it will be worth it in the long run. Take the time to show new female martial artists the ropes. Give them the benefit of your insight. And consider joining organizations that support women in the martial arts. (See Part 8, Chapter 32 for further information.)

DEVELOPING PHYSICAL CONFIDENCE

Developing the confidence to yell loudly without inhibition can be fun and rewarding. It can also help you learn to do your techniques with confidence. Doing techniques well requires the right speed, timing and power — none of which you'll have if you're tentative or unsure. Make a commitment to the technique — even if you do end up executing it incorrectly. Any instructor would rather see an incorrectly performed low block done with enthusiasm than a perfectly done low block performed slowly with little confidence. Even if the enthusiastic low block isn't perfect, it has a much better chance of being successful and doing what it is supposed to do (i.e., block the low section from attack) than a block correctly done with little interest or effort.

Because Tae Kwon Do relies heavily on kicks, much of the time is spent learning how to jump in the air, spin, balance on one foot, and so forth. People fall down while doing this. At first, lower belts feel very embarrassed when they fall down while practicing a kick. But we always say (and mean), "If you're not falling down a lot, you're not trying hard enough." If you commit to your techniques so much that you sometimes fall down trying to kick higher, faster or stronger, you're on the right track. If you never make such mistakes, you're either so vastly talented that this book is completely unnecessary for you, or you aren't trying hard enough. You want to reach perfection even in practice; you should be unwilling to settle for what is simply comfortable. It isn't practice that makes perfect, but perfect practice that makes perfect, as so many sports philosophers have pointed out. But unless you're constantly attempting to outdo and challenge yourself, you aren't practicing perfectly. The martial arts are the one place where you can try and fail and try and fail and no one even notices the failing — just the trying.

Women, especially those who have not been athletic in the past, do bring more self-consciousness to martial arts than men do. They are also much harder on themselves than men are, wanting to do things correctly, right away, immediately. This can be frustrating. It can also be discouraging. Just remember the martial arts are about you becoming better than you were — and it takes time and effort for that to happen.

A good martial artist isn't necessarily one with an awesome roundhouse kick. It might be someone who can coach amazingly, so that others who wouldn't believe it possible can do awesome roundhouse kicks. Every person finds her place in the martial arts, maybe not as the superstar who impresses everyone, but maybe as the one who perseveres and inspires others to follow suit.

Martial arts are about growing and becoming more fit, more flexible, and stress free. This only works when you release your self-criticism and enjoy what you can do and what you do well. This doesn't mean we should not be critical of ourselves or that we don't need to strive for improvement. It simply means we should give ourselves a chance and not write ourselves off too early in the game.

ADJUSTING TO CONTACT

In the beginning, physical contact may be difficult, not because it is physically painful, but because mentally, emotionally, psychologically we're not prepared for physical contact except of a gentler sort. Getting hit violates our sense of space. It makes us feel invaded and vulnerable.

It is important in these first few experiences of physical contact to feel safe. It's OK to tell your partner, "I'm not comfortable with that level of contact," or to say, "Let's take this more slowly." Some people just manage faster and some people aren't bothered at all by the physicality. Fear of contact, of course, is not simply a woman's problem. It can intimidate men as well.

The main problem is we don't know what to expect. And we don't know what to do. As usual, you simply need practice. Give yourself time and permission to be distressed. It's part of the process. Then, when you're no longer affected by the contact, don't forget what it was like when you first started. This empathy will help other martial artists who come up through the ranks after you. Whether they're adults or children, female or male, they'll be happy to have your understanding.

Physical contact requires getting used to, so spend time doing it under controlled conditions. Have a friend grab your wrist while you practice a self-defense technique. Have your partner do a (gentle) chokehold while you decide what techniques can be used to your advantage. The more you work with people who are touching, grappling, grabbing or punching you, the more at ease you'll become.

Another advantage to working with a wide variety of people is that you'll become used to many different methods of attack and you'll learn many different methods of defense and counterattack. Often, we're taught techniques that would work well if we were men fighting other men. However, we are not. As a general rule, women do not get attacked by other women who plan to mug them. Women get attacked by men. Men tend to be taller and heavier than women, so instead of spending your time training to fight someone your own size, train to fight someone a lot bigger than you are.

Training does not mean that we can be reckless and cavalier, certain of our ability to confront and destroy all attackers. It doesn't mean that a man won't succeed in hurting us if he tries. What it does mean is that he'll have more broken ribs after we're through than he had before.

While overcoming the mental blocks about taking hits, we have another difficulty to overcome — hitting other people. Most women simply haven't gotten into fistfights. They may have been hit or slapped before, but they probably haven't punched back. For many women, this is even tougher than getting hit. Ultimately, this stems from a lack of confidence: maybe you'll hurt someone, maybe you'll make someone mad, maybe you'll look foolish, maybe you'll hurt yourself, maybe you don't have what it takes to be a good martial artist, and if you really gave everything your best shot and found out you weren't good enough — what then?

Knowing how to punch another person, even a person you know and like, such as your sparring partner, is a wonderful skill. Who knows how many abusive relationships would never have gotten started if when he threw that first punch she'd blocked and countered hard to the solar plexus. Or the groin. Or how many date rapes could be avoided if when she said no, she had an elbow smash to the nose all ready to go.

But the martial arts aren't just about what physical confrontations might happen someday. There's a whole lot more to it, as you'll discover. Once you become confident of your physical skills, you'll discover mental and emotional changes as well. You'll find yourself becoming a better person, braver and stronger in many ways. You just have to stick with it, even at those times when it seems overwhelming.

31
CONCLUSION

Once you've started on your martial arts journey, you'll be changed forever. You'll become more confident and stronger. You might meet new friends and attempt new challenges. Whatever the journey has in store for you, now is the time to get started. It doesn't matter if you're overweight, or out of shape (although you should always check with your doctor before starting an execise program), you can see immediate benefits when you practice the martial arts.

With dedication and practice, you can become a highly skilled practitioner of Tae Kwon Do. By practicing Tae Kwon Do at least three days a week, you'll be the equivalent of a brown belt in a year. By then, you'll be able to move on to more advanced techniques. Even so, the basic and intermediate techniques shown here take literally a lifetime to master, as there is always a way to do a technique more perfectly.

Tae Kwon Do practice will make you stronger and more confident in many ways, able to meet the challenges of the training hall and the world outside it. Although the keys to Tae Kwon Do include physical skills, such as developing strength and speed, the mental skills you learn, such as working with confidence, should not be regarded lightly. Further, emotional skills, such as those outlined in the Five Tenets, are essential to a deeper understanding of Tae Kwon Do. Only by living with courtesy, integrity, perseverance, self-control and indomitable spirit will a fighter become a true martial artist.

The study of Tae Kwon Do goes beyond mere self-defense. The purpose of Tae Kwon Do lies inside, for as you practice, you will seek self-understanding and enlightenment. It may be a difficult journey, but one that is worth every step of the way.

32
RESOURCES

CLOTHING AND EQUIPMENT

To find any special clothing or equipment you might need, try *The Black Book: The Martial Arts Supplies Guide and Master's Desk Reference.* Available on most newsstands.

Call or write the following martial arts supply companies (some have websites). They carry clothing and equipment for women:

Century Martial Art Supply
1705 National Blvd, Midwest City, OK 73110-7942
(405) 732-2226 • www.centuryma.com

Kwon, Inc.
3755 Broadmoor, SE, Grand Rapids, MI 49512
www.kwon.com

Asian World of Martial Arts
11601 Caroline Road, Philadelphia, PA 19154-2177
(800) 345-2962 • www.awma.com.

Macho Products, Inc.
10045 102nd Terrace, Sebastien, FL 32958
(800) 327-6812 • www.macho.com.

Pil Sung Martial Art Supply
6300 Ridglea Place, Suite 1008, Fort Worth, TX 76116
(817) 738-5408 • www.pil-sung.com

Health in Balance
Supplies especially for women
647 Hillsborough Street, Oakland, CA 94606
(510) 452-2990 • www.home.earthlink.net/~healthbalanc/

Ask your instructor for any catalogs he or she may have; many supply houses have women's stuff in stock, even though they don't advertise it.

ORGANIZATIONS AND ASSOCIATIONS

Now that it is no longer unusual to see women practicing the martial arts, there are more associations and groups that help support them.

The National Women's Martial Arts Federation can help you feel less isolated. They hold training camps and seminars. P.O. Box 44433, Detroit, MI 48244-0433. www.nwmaf.org.

Association of Women Martial Arts Instructors P.O. Box 7033, Houston, TX 77248. http://members.aol.com/AWMAI/home.html.

INDEX